TO:

FROM:

DATE:

Longing for HOME

52 Devotional Reflections on the Hope of Heaven

KATE MOTAUNG

Christian Art PUBLISHERS

Visit Christian Art Gifts, Inc., at www.christianartgifts.com.

Longing for Home: 52 Devotional Reflections on the Hope of Heaven

Published by Christian Art Gifts, Inc., Bloomingdale, IL, USA.

This author is represented by Tim J. Beals, Credo Communications, LLC, https://www.credocommunications.net/.

First edition 2025.

Designed by Christian Art Gifts, Inc.

Cover and interior images used under license from Shutterstock.com.

ISBN 979-8-89678-190-5

Printed in China.

30 29 28 27 26 25
10 9 8 7 6 5 4 3 2 1

For Dani, my friend
who made it home to glory
on September 11, 2024
at age thirty-two

For Rosbin, my son's friend
who made it home to glory
on October 19, 2024
at age nineteen

For Hunter, my friend's son
who made it home to glory
on November 14, 2024
at age nine

Each in your own significant way,
thank you for showing me how to be ready.

ENDORSEMENTS

Few books encompass the longing for and belonging of home—the place you feel safe, seen, and loved by God and others. Kate Motaung's newest book, *Longing for Home,* is a gift of beauty and belonging, perfect for curling up with to shelter you from life's chaos or for giving to someone who needs the grounding assurance of God's presence and care in their life. Motaung's books are known for their gentle, come-alongside spirit. This one is her best yet.

—Brenda L. Yoder, LMHC, award-winning author of *Uncomplicated: Simple Secrets for a Compelling Life*

With tender insight and unwavering biblical truth, Kate Motaung invites us to sit with the ache we all feel—and gently lifts our eyes toward Jesus. *Longing for Home* is not just a devotional; it's a soul-balm for anyone who is weary of the brokenness and hungry for heaven. These pages stirred my heart with hope and reminded me that one day, every ache will be answered with the words we were made to hear: "Welcome Home."

—Lee Nienhuis, author, Bible teacher, and global worker longing for Home

I've long wondered about heaven. When life gets busy and I'm hopping from one daily challenge to the next, where does heaven fit in? Is it relevant? How should it color the way I view my life here on earth? With this book, Kate Motaung has shown me that heaven isn't actually the question; it's the answer. Each devotion opens my eyes to view everyday experiences through an eternal lens—not in a way that induces guilt or condemnation but rather an *invitation* to live with deeper purpose. What a gift this book is. I want to place one in every woman's hands.

—Becky Kopitzke, author of
The SuperMom Myth and *The Cranky Mom Fix*

Kate has done it again. Through devotions steeped in Scripture, *Longing for Home* pulls back the curtains to fix our eyes on eternity. Whether you ardently await heaven or it feels far away or fearful, these devotions are packed with gentle reminders to realign our lives and hope to the reality of our heavenly home. What could be better than heaven? Page after page, you'll discover even the most broken and beautiful moments here will be far eclipsed by what God has prepared for us ahead.

—Lisa Appelo, author of *Life Can Be Good Again: Putting Your World Back Together After It All Falls Apart*

Do you long for home? Do you crave refuge or rest or belonging? This beautifully written book invites you to consider not only what home is, but with *Whom* our home lies.

Through stories of family, loss, and fleeting comforts, Kate lifts our eyes beyond tidy houses and homey places to the only home that can never break or fade. If you feel homesick in your own home, or you long for something you can't name, *Longing for Home* will help you put words to the ache, and point you to the One who is preparing you a home that will last forever.

—Shannon Popkin, author of several books, including
Shaped by God's Promises: Lessons from Sarah on Fear and Faith

TABLE OF CONTENTS

INTRODUCTION

When my mom died of cancer at fifty-nine years old, I had every confidence that by God's grace, she was with the Lord. He had given her a vibrant, vocal faith, and she clung to Him as her life preserver—for this life and the next.

I had been a Christian for several years before my mom passed away, and yet it was only after she died that I really started to think more about heaven and eternity. I missed my mom so much, and my desire to go to heaven increased after she died because I knew she was there.

Then the Lord convicted me with this thought: Why was it that my appetite and anticipation for heaven only increased after I knew my mom was there? Why didn't I have a desperate desire for eternity simply and purely because *God Himself* is there? Shouldn't His presence alone be enough for me? Consider this challenging question from John Piper:

> If you could have heaven, with no sickness, and with all the friends you ever had on earth, and all the food you ever liked, and all the leisure activities you ever enjoyed, and all the natural beauties you ever saw, all the physical pleasures you ever tasted, and no human conflict or any natural disasters, could you be satisfied with heaven, if Christ were not there?[1]

At the risk of sounding dramatic, I realized I had made my mom into an idol of sorts. I had elevated her above my love for the Lord. I asked the Lord to reshape my thinking and the desires of my heart, and to grow my longing for Him and His presence.

My prayer is that God would use the devotions in this book to:

1) Show us how and where we might have elevated aspects of this temporary life over and above our love for Him; and
2) Increase our desire to be at home with the Lord in glory.

As Elyse Fitzpatrick points out, "What is the joy of heaven? Listen, we could have all the beauties of a New Heaven and a New Earth, with creation remade and resurrected bodies, but none of that would be satisfying without *him*."[2]

* * *

As a point of clarification before we begin, I realize there are numerous interpretations and views about the end times. This book is not a study of eschatology (what the Bible teaches about the end times). For the purpose of our time together, we'll be working from three primary beliefs:

1) When believers die, they will be with the Lord immediately (see Jesus' comment to the thief on the cross in Luke 23:42-43).
2) Jesus Christ will come again to judge the living and the dead (2 Tim. 4:1; 1 Pet. 4:5), and to gather all believers to Himself (John 14:1-3; 1 Thess. 4:16-17).
3) God will create a new heavens and a new earth (Isa. 65:17; Rev. 21:1), where He will dwell with His people forever (Rev. 21:3).

When I use the phrase "heaven" or "eternity" in the following pages, please try not to get caught up in whether I'm referring to an "immediate heaven" or the eventual new heavens and new earth. My primary focus is that believers will enter into eternal life after they die and will dwell in the presence of the Lord forever.

When I use the word "we," I'm (most often) referring to those who have acknowledged their sin before God and confessed that Jesus Christ is Lord by placing their faith, trust, and hope in Him for the forgiveness of their sins and the salvation of their souls.

If you haven't done that yet, or you're not sure whether you're a child of God or whether you're going to heaven when you die, I encourage you to take time to think about the following verses and ask the Lord to make Himself known to you:

> "For all have sinned and fall short of the glory of

God, and all are justified freely by his grace through the redemption that came by Christ Jesus." (Rom. 3:23-24 NIV)

"For God so loved the world, that he gave his only Son, that whoever believes in him should not perish but have eternal life." (John 3:16)

"If you confess with your mouth that Jesus is Lord and believe in your heart that God raised him from the dead, you will be saved." (Rom. 10:9)

"Believe in the Lord Jesus, and you will be saved." (Acts 16:31)

"But God, being rich in mercy, because of the great love with which he loved us, even when we were dead in our trespasses, made us alive together with Christ. … For by grace you have been saved through faith. And this is not your own doing; it is the gift of God, not a result of works, so that no one may boast." (Eph. 2:4-5, 8-9)

1

DEFINING HOME

And I heard a loud voice from the throne saying, "Behold, the dwelling place of God is with man. He will dwell with them, and they will be his people, and God himself will be with them as their God."

REVELATION 21:3

Where is home for you?

I posed this question to members of my Bible study group in South Africa. Going around the circle, I was surprised to learn that only two people out of twelve considered Cape Town, the "Mother City" of South Africa, to be their home. One named Namibia as her home; another was from the States; several counted the Eastern Cape of South Africa as home for them.

But nobody in the group—*nobody*—responded with the word "heaven" as their home.

Ask twelve people to define home, and you will get twelve very different answers. Admittedly, I probably even have twelve different definitions of my *own* when it comes to my personal perception of home.

There are my childhood memories of home, my attempts to establish a home away from home as a new bride, and the current state of chaos that my kids refer to as home.

It's relative, this notion of home.

Not just *any* feather pillow, but *my* feather pillow. The one that lulled me to sleep each night as a young girl on the bottom bunk, body wrapped in a cocoon of untucked flannel sheets.

Not just *any* dining room table, but *our* dining room table. The polished mahogany that we annually blanketed with flour and massaged year after year with wooden rolling pins as we flattened and reshaped mounds of refrigerated Christmas cookie dough.

That patch on the bike path where I biffed on a stick while rollerblading, resulting in my inability to button my jeans for a week due to the bruised, swollen hip bone I had pocketed as a souvenir. That patch on the beach where we used to spread our towels in the dark, lie on our backs with hands folded behind our heads, and breathe in the midsummer meteor showers with oohs and aahs. That patch in the yard where the grass grew untamed in a perfect circle, sheltered by the trampoline under which we hid when the purple martins dive-bombed us in defense of their newly hatched young.

Saturday morning waffles with boysenberry syrup. Hudsonville ice cream. Dad's chop suey. Mom's chocolate chip cookies.

These things, for me, encompass home.

But there's more.

There has to be.

Home cannot be thirty-year-old bunk beds, because not only do I no longer sleep there, my boys have outgrown them too. And while we are still blessed to shower the aging mahogany table with pencil shavings and eraser scraps, the Lord knows that the Christmas cookies and tubs of Hudsonville ice cream don't last longer than the blink of an eye. The Rollerblades that were precarious then would be a death wish now, and the rusty springs of the trampoline disintegrated a lifetime ago.

Things change. Life moves on. Stuff breaks, gets thrown away, disappears.

There has to be more.

What defines home for you?

Is it a specific structure, a farmhouse that has been in the family for generations? Is it a region, a broader area like the East Coast of the US or the Eastern Cape of South Africa that encompasses home for you?

Or, like the Church, is it not about the building at all, but about the people? Are you one who is able to uproot and replant just about anywhere, and still call it "home" because of the loved ones who surround you?

Perhaps the most important question is this: How can we change our thinking in a way that will elevate heaven to the top of our list when we think of home?

In this book, we'll explore several components of the eternal home of the believer in Christ: how we pursue it, how we can prepare for it, how we get there, how our hearts are entwined in it, how we hunger for it, and what it will be like when we arrive. My greatest hope is that each of us will be edified and encouraged to set our minds on things above and live each day in the hope of eternity, to the glory of God.

QUESTION FOR REFLECTION

What defines home for you?

2

BETTER HOMES AND GARDENS

For now we see in a mirror dimly,
but then face to face. Now I know in part;
then I shall know fully, even as I have been fully known.
1 CORINTHIANS 13:12

Stand in any queue at the grocery store, and you'll be bombarded by row after row of headlines shouting boldly for your attention: "12 Ways to Organize Your Space." "Simple Decor Ideas on a Budget." "Turn Your Clutter into Glamor." "Fabulous Kitchen Makeovers."

We all desire nice homes. Homes that do more than offer a solid mattress or a square meal. Homes that are more than color-coordinated crates of organized toys and dusty picture frames lining the kid-smudged walls. We want homes that whisper serenity from the fireplace and respite from the creaky porch swing swaying in the breeze. Homes that stir security into steaming cups of tea and wrap intimacy around tired shoulders like a hand-knit afghan.

I once asked a pool of people, "What qualities make up a good home?" To my delight, I received some wonderful insights (and comical quips) in response. A handful of people voted for food and drink as the sign of a good home, including specifics like "bacon in the pan" and "a good wine cellar." A dad of infant triplets plus a toddler managed to unearth himself from mountains of soiled onesies long enough to answer "laundry" and "more laundry."

Love and forgiveness topped the list. Others responded with words like peace, unity, and trust. Communication, dialogue, understanding. Working together, acceptance, and discipline. Fun, shared laughs, and a good sense of humor that pervades. An inviting, calm atmosphere. A place of encouragement and hospitality. Consistency and steadiness. Putting others first. Humility and honesty. Kindness. Respect. Grace. A place where people pray together, and where God is the Lord of each life.

These are beautiful word pictures.

Some of my favorite descriptions could be grouped into the phrases "a place of refuge from the storms of life" and "a soft place to land."

The response that hit home for me?

"They should feel like their home is a haven."

Who *doesn't* want their home to be a haven?

And guess what? All of these descriptions and cherished qualities are components that we *will* find one day in our true home—only to an infinitely magnified degree. Heaven will be all that we desire in a good home, and more. (Well, maybe with the exception of laundry and more laundry—after all, Revelation 21:27 says that "nothing unclean will ever enter it"—now isn't *that* a pleasant thought?)

You want love in your home? What more glorious thought than to dwell forever in the presence of Love Himself (1 John 4:8)? And what is heaven, but a place of complete and utter peace? For there shall be "no more death or mourning or crying or pain" (Rev. 21:4 NIV).

Even those desiring bacon in the pan and a good wine cellar will not be disappointed, should their names be engraved on a place card at the table:

> On this mountain the LORD Almighty will prepare
> **a feast of rich food for all peoples,**
> **a banquet of aged wine—**
> **the best of meats and the finest of wines.**
> On this mountain he will destroy
> the shroud that enfolds all peoples,
> the sheet that covers all nations;
> **he will swallow up death forever.**
> **The Sovereign LORD will wipe away the tears**
> **from all faces;**
> he will remove his people's disgrace
> from all the earth.
> (Isa. 25:6-8 NIV, emphasis added in bold)

Do you long for consistency and steadiness? Heaven does not change. It will not keep us fearfully wondering what will come next, for "Jesus Christ is the same yesterday and today and forever" (Heb. 13:8).

Google's Oxford Languages dictionary defines *refuge* as "a condition of being safe or sheltered from pursuit, danger, or trouble." The same source defines *haven* as "a place of safety or refuge." Can you think of a better shelter or place of safety than the only place where Satan doesn't roam?

The next time you find yourself standing in the checkout line with a screaming toddler stomping all over your cart full of groceries, and you're lamenting over the fact that you can't even afford the magazine, let alone the nifty DIY projects they promise will make your home so much better—let the headlines remind you of the greatest home of all. And best of all, it is already paid for in full by the blood of the Lamb for those who repent and believe.

QUESTION FOR REFLECTION

Which aspects of heaven are you most looking forward to?

3

THE PURSUIT OF HOME

Not that I have already obtained this or am already perfect, but I press on to make it my own, because Christ Jesus has made me his own. Brothers, I do not consider that I have made it my own. But one thing I do: forgetting what lies behind and straining forward to what lies ahead, I press on toward the goal for the prize of the upward call of God in Christ Jesus.

PHILIPPIANS 3:12-14

In an introduction to the classic book *Anne of Green Gables,* by L. M. Montgomery, Jack Zipes writes this:

> Montgomery has touched our imaginations with her creation of Anne, just as Anne touches everyone with whom she comes into contact in the idyllic community of Avonlea. Once touched, we shall keep on reaching out to her because she keeps alive something that we sorely need if we are to move forward in the pursuit of home.[3]

The pursuit of home. What is that? How do we move forward in it? What did it mean for Anne of Green Gables? What does it mean for you?

Let's face it. We pursue a lot of things in this world.

Too many things. We scurry around like ants, up and down grocery aisles, in and out of the office, into the car, out of the car.

We pursue happiness. A future spouse. Parenthood.

We pursue attention. Titles. Qualifications.

We pursue money. Status. Comfort.

We pursue peace. Health. Equality.

Many of these are admirable goals to desire and seek to attain. But what ought to be our *ultimate* pursuit? In a sermon entitled "Home at Last!," J. C. Ryle observed:

> Go, build your happiness on earth, if you are so disposed; choose everything you can fancy would make life enjoyable. Take money, house, and lands; take learning, health and beauty; take honor, rank, obedience, troops of friends; take everything your mind can picture to itself or your eye desire. Take all, and yet I dare to tell you even then you would not find rest. I know well that a few short years, and your heart's confession would be, it is all hollow, empty, and unsatisfying; it is all weariness and disappointment; it is all vanity and vexation of spirit. I know well you would feel within a hungering and famine, a leanness and barrenness of soul; and ready indeed would you be to bear your testimony to the mighty truth: This earth is not our rest.[4]

This earth is not our rest. Have you been trying to make it so? Have your pursuits, like Ryle mentioned in the quote above, left you hollow, empty, and unsatisfied? Or are you pressing forward to attain that perfect rest?

St. Augustine said it best when he wrote, “Thou hast made us for Thyself and our hearts are restless till they rest in Thee.”[5]

It occurs to me that I may only obtain the object of my pursuit when others read about it in the newspaper, as they open the obituaries page one day and read, “Kate Motaung went *home* to be with her Lord and Savior.” Then the pursuit will be over, and I will be *home*.

QUESTION FOR REFLECTION

What are you pursuing and why?

4

THE PURSUIT OF HAPPINESS

You have put more joy in my heart than they have when their grain and wine abound.

PSALM 4:7

The United States Declaration of Independence asserts, "We hold these truths to be self-evident, that all men are created equal, that they are endowed by their Creator with certain unalienable Rights, that among these are Life, Liberty and the pursuit of Happiness." This all sounds well and good—until our pursuit of happiness trumps our pursuit of heaven.

In her book *The Promise Is His Presence*, author Glenna Marshall shares that she used to cringe when she heard the phrase "We're not home yet." She confesses that when she was a child, she used to be afraid of death and Christ's return:

> It wasn't so much the process of dying I was afraid of, or that I wouldn't be part of the resurrected bride of Christ. No, it was less profound than that: I was afraid of what I would miss in my earthly life.
>
> I thought I had a right to enjoy the common human experiences that we look forward to: marriage

> and intimacy, childbirth and parenting, growing in wisdom and milestones. I wanted to die peacefully at a ripe old age with no regrets and nothing to lose. When I had tasted all the goodness of earthly life, *then* I'd be ready for heaven. *Then* I'd be pleased to enjoy what God has to offer.
>
> But that was before I knew the absence of children and the presence of sorrow and physical pain.
>
> Those old fears ruled my thoughts about eternity before I understood that my treasure wasn't actually any of the things that I had hoped would satisfy my longings.[6]

Rebecca Tekautz wrote a convicting and challenging piece in *Relevant* magazine titled "When Happy Trumps Holy." In the article, she makes the following observations about the pursuit of happiness:

> Happiness is our idol. Why are we not pursuing holiness with the same passion with which we are pursuing happiness? How have we come to allow ourselves to put more trust in a fleeting emotion than in a God who says, "Blessed are those who hunger and thirst for righteousness … Blessed are the poor in spirit … Blessed are those who mourn"? …
>
> Happiness is not something to pursue. *Holiness* is something to pursue. …

Christ spent His entire time on earth not teaching us how to be happy, but how to be holy. He is the perfect example of what it looks like to sacrifice humanly happiness for God's holiness. His ragtag group of disciples irritated Him and argued with Him and each other, and He always knew one was destined to betray Him. But He spent time with them anyway, teaching them, loving them, pushing them to grow in holiness. The cross didn't make Him happy, either. Christ was in distress, in pain, and he died.

Between happiness and holiness, Christ chose holy. He chose to make *us* holy.[7]

It's worth mentioning that God is not anti-happiness. Every good thing that we have is from His hand (James 1:17). He blesses us abundantly and beyond measure. His goodness knows no bounds.

Yet, it's possible to so enjoy the earthly, temporal blessings He bestows that we fail to desire the heavenly, lasting blessings. We fix our eyes on what is seen rather than what is unseen. We stuff ourselves with material fare to the point that we have no appetite left over for the delicacies of heaven.

We are yearning for something deeper, something that won't fade like everything we've encountered on this earth. … We long for happiness. I'm not talking about the happiness we feel when we get the

> birthday present we've been hoping for. Or even when we finally meet the *right* person to marry, find a job to invest our lives in, or are in a position to afford the home of our dreams. I'm talking about the happiness that comes from life in the presence of God, where there is nothing but satisfaction, wholeness, love, and holiness.[8]

The pursuit of happiness on earth at the expense of the pursuit of holiness has everything to do with the pursuit of home. What we pursue here and now can and will have eternal consequences. Which happiness are you chasing?

QUESTION FOR REFLECTION

In what ways have you been pursuing your own personal happiness on earth over eternal joy in heaven?

5

A GOAL ATTAINED

I have fought the good fight, I have finished the race, I have kept the faith. Now there is in store for me the crown of righteousness, which the Lord, the righteous Judge, will award to me on that day—and not only to me, but also to all who have longed for his appearing.

2 TIMOTHY 4:7-8 NIV

We chase after numerous pursuits in this lifetime. We may even get so entangled in the worldly rat race that we lose sight of why we're here in the first place.

Consider some common earthly pursuits. Let's take running, for example. Personally, I would never willingly put myself through such torture, but I admire those who are disciplined and fit enough to do so. I know some people who spend hours, days, and weeks training for a specific race. I can imagine the satisfaction that comes when the race day has arrived, and after toil and sweat—and perhaps a desperate prayer or two—you manage to cross the sought-after finish line.

Maybe you've been working on an advanced degree. Night after night, you've pored over the books, doled out thousands of dollars in tuition fees, typed fervently at your computer until every last assignment was submitted. Then you finally obtain that prized piece of paper, indicating your achievement.

It feels good, doesn't it? It is a fulfilling and satisfying thing to realize one's pursuits. If these earthly goals can carry such pleasure, imagine what it will be like when we make it to the end of the all-important race. When we get that one certificate that really matters. When we arrive at the goal of our faith, the salvation of our souls. When we lay down our man-made trophies and pick up the crown of life. When we, Lord willing, hear the words, "Well done, good and faithful servant" (Matt. 25:21).

As the apostle Paul says in 1 Corinthians 9:24-25 (NIV), "Do you not know that in a race all the runners run, but only one gets the prize? Run in such a way as to get the prize. Everyone who competes in the games goes into strict training. They do it to get a crown that will not last, but we do it to get a crown that will last forever."

It is purely by His help and sustaining grace that we could ever attain such a goal—not by our own works, but by the grace of God Himself. And certainly it will not be due to our own accomplishments, but solely because of the One who hung on the cross and declared, "It is finished" (John 19:30).

We won't be patting ourselves on the back that day for a job well done, but rather praising the One who began a good work and was faithful to complete it (Phil. 1:6). What joy will fill our hearts when we come to the end of this journey and reach our final destination. Only then will we be home, sweet home.

QUESTION FOR REFLECTION

Which pursuits in your life do you consider worthwhile, and why? What is your primary pursuit?

6

HOME FROM EXILE

And if I go and prepare a place for you, I will come back and take you to be with me that you also may be where I am.

JOHN 14:3 NIV

In his compilation of daily devotional meditations, *Morning and Evening*, Charles Spurgeon eloquently expressed the following:

> To come to thee is to come home from exile, to come to land out of the raging storm, to come to rest after long labour, to come to the goal of my desires and the summit of my wishes. But Lord, how can a stone rise, how can a lump of clay come away from the horrible pit? O raise me, draw me. Thy grace can do it. Send forth thy Holy Spirit to kindle sacred flames of love in my heart, and I will continue to rise until I leave life and time behind me, and indeed come away.[9]

What is worth noting from the excerpt above is how Spurgeon was aware that he was wholly incapable of pursuing heaven apart from the Spirit of God. It's impossible for us to pursue our own reservation in the heavenly mansions, or to purchase our right to be there.

No earthly efforts can earn us a place in paradise of our own accord.

Yet we can receive a permanent residence in this matchless abode called heaven, through the blood of Jesus Christ, and this gift is freely available to all who believe. "But to all who did receive him, who believed in his name, he gave the right to become children of God, who were born, not of blood nor of the will of the flesh nor of the will of man, but of God" (John 1:12-13).

After this right has been granted, the pursuit is on. We can't purchase a table in heaven, but once the reservation has been made, we can strive toward it as our final destination. Since God Himself, the owner of the establishment, has called ahead to make the booking, we can have full assurance that once we arrive at the entrance, our names will be on the reservation list, engraved in the Book of Life. We shall not be turned away, but will sit down to feast with the King of kings.

This is the difference between *justification* and *sanctification*. We can't make the reservation in eternity for ourselves; but once it has been made, we press on and pursue it with all godliness and holiness. The apostle Paul describes this pursuit well:

> Not that I have already obtained this or am already perfect, but **I press on to make it my own, because Christ Jesus has made me his own.** Brothers, I do not consider that I have made it my own. But one thing I do: forgetting what lies behind and straining

> forward to what lies ahead, I press on toward the goal for the prize of the upward call of God in Christ Jesus. (Phil. 3:12-14, emphasis added in bold)

May the Lord give us the grace and strength to keep pressing on toward the goal until He comes back to usher us home.

QUESTION FOR REFLECTION

In what ways or areas of your life have you been trying to pursue God in your own strength?

7

THE ONLY ROAD HOME

"And you know the way to where I am going." Thomas said to him, "Lord, we do not know where you are going. How can we know the way?" Jesus said to him, "I am the way, and the truth, and the life. No one comes to the Father except through me."

JOHN 14:4-6

In the ten years I spent living in South Africa, I took many routes home. Granted, the departure always originated from the same airport, but the itineraries and layovers I experienced when traveling from Cape Town to Grand Rapids, Michigan were as varied as the number of passport stamps I collected. I've strolled for hours through the corridors of the Amsterdam airport, heavily burdened by an overstuffed backpack. I've snatched sleep atop bulging bags sprawled across the unfriendly chairs in Frankfurt. I've paid British pounds for an overpriced toasted panini at Heathrow and divided it into five pieces when my family and I ran out of snacks. I've gone the direct route over the Atlantic, sometimes to Atlanta, sometimes to New York, usually stopping to refuel in Senegal. I've taken shuttles with three children to sleep in unplanned hotels in Cleveland and Chicago.

My routes home are rarely the same. But always—*always*—if I want to get to my final destination, I have to go through Grand Rapids. It's inevitable. I can't avoid it if I want to get home.

It's the same with salvation.

There are many ways we can come to Jesus. Some of us crawl to the cross from the pit of despair. Some of us kneel in the same pew we've warmed for decades. Others have had their eyes opened from a hospital bed minutes before death. But if we want to end up in heaven in the world to come, we can only get there through Jesus Christ.

Allow me to clarify: I'm not saying that there are many roads to heaven. What I'm saying is that there are many ways in which God draws us to Christ. The Lord leads each of us down different paths to bring us to Himself, and ultimately, for the believer, to take us home. But if we want to *get* home, we have to fly via the cross. There's no other way home.

We can't earn our way there. "For by grace you have been saved through faith. And this is not your own doing; it is the gift of God, not a result of works, so that no one may boast" (Eph. 2:8-9). The Scriptures are clear: "Whoever believes in the Son has eternal life; whoever does not obey the Son shall not see life, but the wrath of God remains on him" (John 3:36).

J. C. Ryle gives this challenge:

> The Lord grant you may consider well your own fitness for heaven. There must be a certain meetness for

> that blessed place in our minds and characters. It is senseless, vain, and absurd to suppose that all shall go there, whatever their lives have been. May God the Holy Ghost incline you to examine yourselves faithfully while you have time, before that great day cometh when the unconverted shall be past all hope and the saints past all fear.[10]

What about you? Have you "considered well your own fitness for heaven"? Are you still relying on your own strength, in hopes that the good things you've done in this life will outweigh the bad when you face the Lord in judgment? Isaiah 64:6 (NIV) says, "All of us have become like one who is unclean, and all our righteous acts are like filthy rags; we all shrivel up like a leaf, and like the wind our sins sweep us away."

Without the Holy Spirit as the pacemaker in our beating hearts, all of our righteous acts are like filthy rags to God. We will shrivel up, and our sins will sweep us away. It's a tough reality to face, but if you haven't bowed your knee to Christ as Lord, the future home of heaven will be locked forever to you. You may knock on the door, but no one will let you in.

Just as I could never get home from South Africa without going through Grand Rapids, we will never get home to heaven without faith in Jesus Christ.

QUESTION FOR REFLECTION

Describe the manner in which the Lord drew you to Himself.

8

THE RIGHT FLIGHT

Enter through the narrow gate. For wide is the gate and broad is the road that leads to destruction, and many enter through it. But small is the gate and narrow the road that leads to life, and only a few find it.

MATTHEW 7:13-14 NIV

In December 2023, an unaccompanied six-year-old boy was sent on the wrong flight to visit his grandparents. He was supposed to board a plane to Fort Myers, Florida, and instead, the airline placed him on an aircraft headed to Orlando.[11] In February 2023, a man from New York was trying to visit Sydney, Australia, and accidentally flew to Sidney, Montana.[12] These individuals both entered through the wrong gate, and the mistake had major consequences.

There are few things more frustrating than being stranded in an airport because of a canceled flight and unable to get home. It's happened to me many times. Once, I was on the last leg of a thirty-hour journey, just three short driving hours from my destination. It was a flight that would take less than an hour from takeoff to landing, but the weather was too treacherous to fly.

I was so close, and I couldn't get home.

In 2010, many passengers couldn't reach their destination when an Icelandic volcano caused the visibility of European airspace to be shrouded by a dense ash cloud, grounding flights for weeks.[13] In July 2024, a massive tech outage impacted countless industries, including airlines. Delta canceled more than 6,000 flights. When the outage happened, a man named J. R. Reed had three minor children in three different states who were all unable to get home due to canceled flights and Delta's decision to pause their unaccompanied minors program.[14] Being unable to get home is a helpless, frustrating feeling, isn't it?

If you are a believer in Jesus Christ, you will never face that fear or frustration. He will never allow you to accidentally get on the wrong aircraft. You will never be stuck in an airport for hours or days on end. Not only has Christ purchased a jet to deliver you safely to your destination, He has also pacified the snowstorm of God's wrath and cleared the dense cloud of ash preventing you from being able to glimpse the glory of God. If you are a Christian, He *will* get you home.

But Jesus does clarify that there is only one way to get home to Him. Many go through the wide gate and follow the broad road, but that popular choice leads nowhere good or desirable. In fact, the Bible says it "leads to destruction, and many enter through it" (Matt. 7:13). This may seem harsh, but God's justice is actually a good and necessary aspect of His character and plan.

> Judgment is necessary for justice to be done in the world, and justice must be done if this world, redeemed and renewed, is to be home. God cannot be good if he is not just. …
>
> Judgment is not set aside in God's economy, but neither does it have the last word. According to the Christian gospel, every sinner can flee to the cross of Christ. There, an innocent man was judged in the stead of the guilty, and God's wrath was poured out on his beloved Son. On the cross God made embrace possible rather than exclusion. When we declare faith in Jesus' death and resurrection and anticipate his return, when we admit guilt and renounce self-righteousness, we go free.
>
> Because of the cross, wanderers get home.[15]

He has made it possible for us to be sure of our destination, as long as we are in Him. When the final call is made at the boarding gate to eternity, make sure you're flying with the right pilot—the only One who can carry you *home*.

QUESTION FOR REFLECTION

How can you be sure that you're on the narrow road and that you entered through the small gate?

9

LOST WITHOUT A MAP

You make known to me the path of life.

PSALM 16:11

When my daughter Dineo was in seventh grade, she decided to join the cross-country team at her school. She had never run competitively before, but her friends were doing it, so she decided to join the fun. I was late in scheduling the required sports physical exam and couldn't get an appointment with our regular family doctor before the first meet, so I took Dineo to a walk-in clinic to get the necessary forms filled out in time.

During the exam, a doctor we had never met before said he thought he detected a faint heart murmur. He wanted Dineo to see a cardiologist for further testing. It took a while to get an appointment with the specialist, and the first cross-country meet was only a few days away. I asked the doctor if this news meant Dineo shouldn't participate in the meet or run at all until she got the green light from the cardiologist. He replied nonchalantly, "She should be fine."

Should be? That didn't sound very reassuring to me. He looked at my girl and said to her, "Just don't push yourself too hard. If you start to feel pain in your chest or have difficulty breathing, stop running." These words did little to boost my confidence.

Despite my hesitation, I agreed to let her participate in the first meet, which took place at a local vineyard we'd never visited before. The two-mile course weaved in and out of rows of grapevines, almost like a maze. Spectators were unable to see the runners during the race except for a straight, open stretch at the very end.

My husband, boys, and I waited with great anticipation to see Dineo emerge from the vineyard in her final push toward the finish line. The minutes seemed to drag on, then finally we heard the crowd of spectators burst into applause. The lead runners had appeared, giving every ounce of energy they had left to finish well. More and more runners passed by, without any sign of Dineo. Since she had never competed before, I had no idea how her pace compared to others on the team or what a "normal" time would be for her. Still, the minutes ticked by with no sign of her. Then we overheard runners who had finished the race saying that there was a swarm of bees on the course, and that several racers had been stung multiple times.

I started to worry. Had she been stung by bees and experienced an allergic reaction to the stings? Had she pushed herself too hard with an undiagnosed heart murmur and passed out on the course without anyone around to see her?

The last of the runners came and went, and spectators started packing up their belongings and loading their cars.

I turned at my husband. "Should we go look for her?"

Just as I was about to head into the vineyard myself in search of my missing girl, she emerged from the grapevines—healthy and well. She took one look at the finish line and sprinted toward it. After she finished the race, we asked her, "What happened?"

"I got lost," she explained. Apparently someone had been trying to warn runners of the bees, encouraging them to avoid the swarm by pointing in a certain direction, and Dineo thought they meant she should turn and run the way they were pointing. She got completely turned around and couldn't find any other runners to follow, or a way to get out.

Maybe you feel that way about life in general. As though you followed the wrong directions and got hopelessly lost, with no idea how to escape from the maze. You feel stuck in an overgrown vineyard with no exit signs and no one to show you how to finish the race and get home.

The good news is, there is a way out. God gave us a map in the form of His Word, and it can and does reveal the way to salvation. The Word of God will lead the way home. Don't be lost in the maze of life without it.

QUESTION FOR REFLECTION

When and how have you found direction from God's Word?

10

THE PATH TO HEAVEN

I give them eternal life, and they will never perish,
and no one will snatch them out of my hand.

JOHN 10:28

Not only does the Lord use different means to draw us to Christ, but once we are safely in the palm of His hand, in His providence, He also allows different circumstances to shape and affect us as we wait for eternity with Him.

Cancer. Unemployment. Divorce. Miscarriage. Car accident.

We process and work through these providences in a myriad of ways. Some of us have to endure them personally. Others support from a distance with heart ties and soul sighs.

We can all expect to endure difficult terrain on the journey home. Some will trudge across mile after unending mile of trials and hardships. Think about Christian's journey in John Bunyan's classic, *Pilgrim's Progress.* He met constant challenges once he set his face toward the Celestial City.

The path to heaven is not always smooth sailing. In fact, at times, the storms of life may thrash us about so violently that we feel sure our faith will be shipwrecked before we reach the shore. Some days, the thunder and rain are so loud and the sky is so dark, we struggle to hear His voice or see His hand at work. It can be tempting to question whether God is still there. Perhaps you've considered giving up on the Christian faith altogether.

The first time my mom was diagnosed with cancer, my faith faltered. I asked myself whether following Christ was worth it, even if believers and unbelievers alike faced similar hardships. What's the point? I wondered. Then the Lord brought to mind a passage from Scripture when "many of [Jesus'] disciples turned back and no longer walked with Him. So Jesus said to the twelve, 'Do you want to go away as well?' Simon Peter answered Him, 'Lord, to whom shall we go? You have the words of eternal life'" (John 6:66-68). I realized in that moment that there was nowhere else to go; He alone was my only hope.

Consider the following excerpt from Charles Spurgeon's *Morning and Evening*. It's a devotional written on the words, "able to keep you from falling" from Jude 24:

> In one sense, the path to heaven is very safe. But in other respects, there is no road as dangerous. It is surrounded by difficulties—one false step (and how easy it is to take that false step if we are outside of God's grace!), and down we go.
>
> … We have many enemies who will try to push us down. The road is certainly rough and we are certainly weak—but in addition to this, enemies lurk

> in ambush, rushing out when we least expect them, hoping to trip us up or hurl us over the nearest cliff. Only an almighty arm can preserve us from these unseen foes who seek to destroy us. That kind of arm is engaged for our defense. "He who promised is faithful" (Hebrews 10:23), and He is able to keep us from stumbling.[16]

I thank the Lord that no matter what happens—even on those days when I doubt His goodness and presence—He will indeed hold me fast. What a comfort to know that despite all the obstacles of life, all the hurdles and dangers that may frustrate our walk, nothing can separate us from the love of Christ (Rom. 8:35-39). Those whom Christ has prepared for glory cannot be snatched from His hand (John 10:28).

QUESTION FOR REFLECTION

Describe a time in your life when you were tempted to believe that your circumstances might disqualify you from heaven, or when you wondered if Jesus would let you out of His grip.

11

PAID IN FULL

And you, who were dead in your trespasses and the uncircumcision of your flesh, God made alive together with him, having forgiven us all our trespasses, by canceling the record of debt that stood against us with its legal demands. This he set aside, nailing it to the cross.

COLOSSIANS 2:13-14

One month after my aunt and uncle made the final payment on the twenty-year mortgage on their home, they threw a huge party, including catering, live music, and a covered wooden stage that my uncle built by hand for the band. Having a home that was paid in full and officially and completely belonged to them was a big deal and worth celebrating.

For many years, my mother-in-law's house was in my husband's name. She lived there; he didn't. It was *her* house, but it was in *his* name. There was great delight and a sense of accomplishment when the final mortgage payment was submitted, and the house was paid in full.

Similarly, the earthly tents in which we live, our bodies, are our individual dwellings, yet they have *His* name written all over them. If we have trusted in Jesus, then the Holy Spirit dwells with us in our hearts. The greatest delight is that Jesus has already paid in full for a home that will never perish, spoil, or fade (1 Pet. 1:4 NIV). This great truth should cause us to live lives that reflect our gratitude for the eternal home that has been prepared for us.

Before we receive Christ, we are burdened by an immeasurable weight of sin that we cannot possibly pay back ourselves. It is like having a zillion-dollar mortgage. We could never pay the immense debt. And yet in Colossians, the apostle Paul tells us that Jesus Christ canceled "the record of debt that stood against us with its legal demands" (Col. 2:14). It's gone. Wiped clean. Nothing more is owed. Through His death and resurrection, He has forgiven all our sins and nailed our debt to the cross. Hallelujah, right?

In 2022, President Joe Biden announced a student debt relief plan that was supposedly going to clear or at least diminish the college tuition debts owed by a certain group of individuals. I was not in the group that was supposed to benefit, but after spending ten years paying off loans for my own college education, I can imagine the relief I would've felt if someone in authority made a sweeping declaration that my debt had been wiped away. No more burden!

And yet the clearing of our spiritual debt is infinitely greater and more significant than a five- or six-figure college loan debt.

In his classic *The Pilgrim's Progress*, John Bunyan depicts the moment that the main character, Christian, loses the heavy burden of sin he has been carrying his whole life:

> So I saw in my dream, that just as Christian came up with the cross, his burden loosed from off his shoulders, and fell from off his back, and began to tumble, and so continued to do till it came to the mouth of the sepulchre, where it fell in, and I saw it no more.
>
> Then was Christian glad and lightsome, and said with a merry heart, "He hath given me rest by his sorrow, and life by his death." Then he stood still a while, to look and wonder; for it was very surprising to him that the sight of the cross should thus ease him of his burden.[17]

"The sight of the cross." Have you experienced that feeling, when you knew the weight of your burden had been lifted from your back and removed forever? That's what Christ has done through His death on the cross, and that's the reason we can have hope for eternal life with Him.

QUESTION FOR REFLECTION

Write or say a prayer of gratitude to the Lord for removing your burden of sin for all time.

12

A HOME PREPARED

Therefore, preparing your minds for action, and being sober-minded, set your hope fully on the grace that will be brought to you at the revelation of Jesus Christ.

1 PETER 1:13

In his book *Heaven*, Randy Alcorn gives the analogy of astronauts who have prepared and trained for a five-year mission to Mars. Alcorn writes about how ludicrous it would be for those astronauts to lift off, then ask each other, "What do you know about Mars?" One astronaut looks blankly at the other, then admits: "Nothing. We never talked about it. I guess we'll find out when we get there."[18]

Of course they would have studied, researched, and prepared for their destination before climbing into the spaceship. How much more should we, as heaven-bound saints, be preparing ourselves for our landing in the Celestial City after liftoff from this planet? As Alcorn comments, "It's inconceivable that your training would not have included extensive study of and preparation for your ultimate destination."[19]

How are you preparing for your ultimate destination?

I found the following excerpt to be very challenging

and thought-provoking. It comes from the book *Relationships: A Mess Worth Making*, by Timothy Lane and Paul Tripp.

> How do you stimulate your imagination in any area of life? If you have a vision for decorating your house, you buy decorating magazines and pore over them until you get an idea of what you want to do. If you want to take a vacation, you sit down with someone who has been where you want to go. You talk about his trip, gaining insight and excitement about what you can do when you get there. You will probably get travel brochures or look at the pictures from your friend's trip.[20]

There may not be any travel brochures or web pages offered by those who've been to heaven already—except for one: the testimony of Christ Himself. He is the friend who shows us the pictures of His trip, who describes the beach house at the end of the winding dirt road, who provides us with full-color magazine images to gawk at and drool over.

As Alcorn suggests in his book *In Light of Eternity*, "If you want your children or grandchildren to be more excited about heaven than the Grand Canyon or Disney World or summer camp, open up the Bible and talk to them about heaven's attractions, not just earth's."[21] We have sixty-six books in the Bible to stir our hearts and increase our desire for the greatest holiday destination imaginable. To quote C. S. Lewis's description of our arrival, "The term is over: the holidays have begun."[22] Are you ready for the holidays to begin?

Joni Eareckson Tada says, "Heaven may be as near as next year, or next week; so it makes good sense to spend some time here on earth thinking candid thoughts about that marvelous future reserved for us."[23] Unlike a vacation or a mission to Mars, we don't know when our departure date will be. We would be wise to be well prepared.

If heaven is our true, eternal home, and heaven is where we're headed, then surely we ought to prepare ourselves for our final destination, the mansion that is prepared for us. But how exactly can we prepare ourselves for that glorious place? We'll consider one way in the next entry.

QUESTION FOR REFLECTION

In what ways are you actively preparing for your eternal destination?

13

REPAIRING RELATIONSHIPS

If it is possible, as far as it depends on you, live at peace with everyone.

ROMANS 12:18 NIV

One practical way we can prepare ourselves for heaven is by making sure all of our relationships are intact. While we can't take any material things with us when we die, human souls are eternal.

In the Gospel of Matthew, Jesus instructs His disciples, "So if you are offering your gift at the altar and there remember that your brother has something against you, leave your gift there before the altar and go. First be reconciled to your brother, and then come and offer your gift" (Matt. 5:23-24). In other words, if you realize that someone is upset with you or may be holding a grudge against you, or if you have a relationship that needs repairing, make it a priority to go and do all that you can to restore that relationship.

Having said this, I realize that face-to-face reconciliation is not always possible. There may be times or circumstances in which it would be unwise (or just plain impossible) to pursue direct communication. In those cases, I encourage you to still take time to pray Psalm

139:23-24 (NIV): "Search me, God, and know my heart; test me and know my anxious thoughts. See if there is any offensive way in me, and lead me in the way everlasting." Ask the Lord to reveal to you any unresolved interpersonal issues that may be hindering your relationship with Him.

Ask Him to help you "get rid of all bitterness, rage and anger, brawling and slander, along with every form of malice" (Eph. 4:31 NIV). Instead, pray that the Lord would give you the grace and strength to "be kind and compassionate to one another, forgiving each other, just as in Christ God forgave you" (Eph. 4:32 NIV).

Humbling yourself and taking the first step to repair a damaged relationship can speak volumes to anyone who witnesses your actions. Not only is it an act of obedience, it is also an imitation of God's actions toward us, as He did not wait for us to apologize or ask for forgiveness before He pursued us. "While we were still sinners, Christ died for us" (Rom. 5:8 NIV).

Perhaps there was a time when you spoke harshly to someone or treated them unkindly. You knew in your heart it was wrong at the time, but you never went to them afterwards to apologize or seek forgiveness. Maybe your actions offended someone (either intentionally or unintentionally). Perhaps you and a friend had a misunderstanding that led to a rift in your relationship, or maybe they made a choice you disagreed with and you distanced yourself from them.

Whatever the case may be, ask the Lord to help you take any necessary steps to do what you can to restore fractured relationships, extend the same forgiveness you have been given in Christ, and "as far as it depends on you, live at peace with everyone" (Rom. 12:18 NIV).

QUESTION FOR REFLECTION

Is the Lord laying any relationships on your heart that need mending? Is He leading you to address any unresolved bitterness you harbor in your heart toward someone?

14

PREPARING FOR HOME

But in keeping with his promise we are looking forward to a new heaven and a new earth, where righteousness dwells. So then, dear friends, since you are looking forward to this, make every effort to be found spotless, blameless and at peace with him.

2 PETER 3:13-14 NIV

In my initial move to South Africa, I only packed the things I thought would be useful to me during my six months in Cape Town. I left behind all the things I thought I wouldn't need or use. In a similar way, as we prepare for our final destination, let's ask God to help us leave behind the things that are not edifying or sanctifying in our journey toward the Celestial City. As the writer of Hebrews exhorts, "let us also lay aside every weight, and sin which clings so closely, and let us run with endurance the race that is set before us, looking to Jesus, the founder and perfecter of our faith, who for the joy that was set before Him endured the cross, despising the shame, and is seated at the right hand of the throne of God" (Heb. 12:1-2).

One way to get ready for heaven is to glorify God by throwing off every weight, burden, and sin that so easily entangles us. Satan would love nothing more than for our vision to be clouded by worldly temptation so our desire to be with God is diminished. We need to ask God, not on a monthly or weekly basis, but on a daily—no, *hourly*—basis to "forgive us our sins and to cleanse us from all unrighteousness" (1 John 1:9). Only through His cleansing grace and forgiveness will this promise come to pass: "Blessed are the pure in heart, for they shall see God" (Matt. 5:8). If any of us wants to see God, if we want to inherit the kingdom of heaven, we would do well to fall on our knees, acknowledge our own spiritual bankruptcy, and cling to the cross. May the following Puritan prayer become ours:

> Thou art my divine treasury in whom all fullness dwells, my life, hope, joy, peace, glory, end; May I be daily more and more conformed to thee, with the meekness and calmness of the Lamb in my soul, and a feeling sense of the felicity of heaven, where I long to join angels free from imperfections, where in me the image of my adored Saviour will be completely restored, so that I may be fit for his enjoyments and employments. I am not afraid to look the king of terrors in the face, for I know that I shall be drawn, not driven, out of the world. Until then let me continually glow and burn out for thee, and when the last great change shall come let me awake in thy likeness, leaving behind me an example that will glorify thee while my spirit rejoices in heaven, and

my memory is blessed upon earth, with those who follow me praising thee for my life.[24]

By God's grace and because of the perfect sacrifice of His Son on the cross, those who trust in Him do not have to fear what will happen after death. Like antsy, impatient children on Christmas Eve, we are looking forward, groaning, waiting with bated breath. But what do we do while we wait? As Peter says, "You ought to live holy and godly lives as you look forward to the day of God and speed its coming" (2 Pet. 3:11-12 NIV).

With the help of the Holy Spirit, we can show our love for God by keeping the commandments found in His Word. As we do so, the reward is that God Himself will come and make His home with us.

QUESTION FOR REFLECTION

How are you making an effort—through the power of the Holy Spirit within you—to be found spotless, blameless, and at peace with God? In what areas of your life might you rely on Him more to help you improve?

15

THINGS ABOVE

Set your minds on things above, not on earthly things.

COLOSSIANS 3:2 NIV

One summer evening, I attended a women's fellowship gathering with some women from my church. About twenty of us sat in lawn chairs in a circle outside, enjoying the July evening breeze. For some reason the conversation turned to loss and death. One woman, who works as a nurse, explained, "In my job, I spend a lot of time with people who are nearing the end of their lives, and I've seen a lot of death. And from what I've witnessed, there isn't much difference in the responses from Christians and unbelievers who are about to die." Around the circle, women were surprised and discouraged—including me. How could that be? What went wrong?

Although I never met any of the individuals she was referring to, I suspect this lack of distinction could be attributed to several factors, including a lack of true understanding of who God is, what He has done, what He has promised, and what lies ahead for His people.

If we truly live out our belief in the gospel, when we near the end of our lives, there should be a marked difference in our demeanor and outlook compared to those who don't know the Lord. We can mourn losses in this life while still clinging fast and testifying to the sure hope of eternal life with the One who has given us every good thing.

In his book *In Light of Eternity*, Randy Alcorn offers a helpful perspective:

> Since Christ came to free us from bondage to the fear of death (Hebrews 2:15), and since death is the necessary doorway to take us to heaven, why is it that so many Christians today are so afraid to die?
>
> The answer is simple—we've made this world our home. We've laid up our treasures on earth. Consequently, since every day brings us closer to our death, every day takes us further from our treasures. We end up backing into eternity, not wanting to let go of all those treasures we've accumulated.
>
> Christ calls us to turn it around. He says to store up our treasures in heaven, not earth. That way, every day that brings us closer to our death brings us closer to our treasures. Instead of backing away from our treasures, we can spend our lives moving toward our treasures.
>
> He who spends his life moving away from his treasures has reason to despair. He who spends his life moving toward his treasures has reason to rejoice.[25]

In his first letter to the Thessalonians, the apostle Paul challenges his listeners (and all believers): "But we do not want you to be uninformed, brothers, about those who are asleep, that you may not grieve as others do who have no hope" (1 Thess. 4:13). If we truly possess the hope we proclaim as believers, the nurses at the hospital should notice a difference.

May God help us to set our minds on things above and to live (and die) in a way that makes others marvel at the grace of God, the light of Christ, and the hope of eternity that radiates from those who are held by Him.

QUESTION FOR REFLECTION

What is keeping you from setting your mind fully on the hope of things above?

TRUSTING THE HOMEOWNER

Do not let your hearts be troubled. You believe in God; believe also in me. My Father's house has many rooms; if that were not so, would I have told you that I am going there to prepare a place for you? And if I go and prepare a place for you, I will come back and take you to be with me that you also may be where I am.

JOHN 14:1-3 NIV

Some friends of ours moved 700 miles across the country to live closer to their parents. Before arriving in their new town, they signed a purchase agreement to buy a home they had never seen. Their parents had viewed the house and sent pictures, but our friends had never been there to see what it was really like. They trusted the opinion of their parents to choose a home for their family.

It's a bit like that for us with heaven, isn't it? None of us have the chance to see heaven before we move there. We know that Jesus has gone ahead to prepare a place for us, but we've never been there ourselves. Yet our all-knowing, all-good heavenly Father has sent us pictures through His Word and His creation to whet our appetite before we move in. Before Jesus went to the cross, He encouraged His disciples with the words quoted at the beginning of this entry. To quote Charles Spurgeon, "Heaven is a prepared place for a prepared people."[26]

What a pleasure to have this promise from the One who created both the heavens and the earth. Like our friends who moved across the country, trusting their parents for a place to live, we can trust the perfect opinion and recommendation of our heavenly Father and can look forward with great anticipation, certain that He will provide the perfect home for us.

I can relate to the sentiments Jen Pollock Michel shared in her book *Keeping Place*: "For as certain as I am about my future home with God, I feel like the bride wearing a blindfold and awaiting her surprise. I don't know what to expect aside from knowing that it will be beyond my asking or imagining."[27]

I confess, I am a planner. I like to know what to expect. If I'm meeting a friend at a restaurant I've never been to before, I look at the menu online ahead of time. If we're traveling to a town we've never visited, I study the route on a map, scope out the destination online, look at any pictures I can find, and research what else is nearby.

When it comes to preparing for eternity with the Lord, I don't have the same luxury of reading reviews from people who have been there before—except, of course, the matchless testimony of the Lord Jesus Himself. And because I trust Him and the nature and character of my Father in heaven, I can rest assured that I will certainly not be disappointed.

In His Sermon on the Mount, Jesus says to His followers, "Which of you, if your son asks for bread, will give him a stone? Or if he asks for a fish, will give him a snake? If you, then, though you are evil, know how to give good gifts to your children, how much more will your Father in heaven give good gifts to those who ask him!" (Matt. 7:9-11 NIV).

Being welcomed into the eternal home that God has prepared for us and dwelling there in His glorious presence is the culmination of all of His good gifts to us—better than anything we've experienced before.

QUESTION FOR REFLECTION

In what ways do you lack trust or faith that the place God has prepared for you is even better than you can imagine?

17

PITCHING TENTS

By faith ... he lived in tents, as did Isaac and Jacob, who were heirs with him of the same promise. For he was looking forward to the city with foundations, whose architect and builder is God.

HEBREWS 11:9-10 NIV

On several occasions I have packed boxes knowing that we were about to move, but not yet aware of where we would be going. It's a bit unsettling, especially for someone who likes to plan ahead and know what's coming. But the Lord has always—*always*—been faithful to provide immeasurably more than all we could ask or imagine (Eph. 3:20-21).

At times, the rental accommodations in which we dwelled felt like tents—sometimes I only unpacked what was necessary for survival. Looking back, I can see God's grace in allowing us to live in such a way. The Lord knows how easily entangled my heart can become in the things of this world. Though I certainly haven't viewed the unknowns with unshakable trust, I now see these uncertainties regarding my earthly future as God's mercy. In His kindness, He provided this fluid and nomadic lifestyle to remind me to hold my earthly treasures loosely—with open, cupped hands.

My immediate family of five is presently residing in the United States, but this country is not home for four out of five of us. My husband and three children were all born under the African sun. They have dug deep of the sub-Saharan soil; its red richness remains tucked away in their hearts and under their fingernails. They have tasted salty splashes along South African coastlines, and it has left them thirsty. Thirsty for home.

While there is much in this leg of the journey that is pleasant and meaningful, my kids and husband long for home. Though the Lord may keep us here for a handful of years, in the grander vision, this is just a pit stop. This reality helps us to remember the same about our entire journey on earth. God may steer us to any number of pit stops along the way—some lasting longer than others. But in the big scheme of things, they're all just temporary.

Three days before my daughter started her second year of college, she landed a spot in an on-campus house instead of the dorm she expected to return to. Since we got the news about the house on short notice, we hadn't planned for all of the kitchen items my daughter would need to stock her kitchen so she could cook meals for herself. The day before she moved in, we made a list and went out together to shop. Many of the items she had used in her dorm the previous year had either been lost, damaged, or broken. It pained me to spend money on new items knowing that they would likely soon succumb to the same fate.

As I drove from one store to the next, I realized again that nothing in this life is meant to last. Like Abraham, we are to be "looking forward to the city with foundations" (Heb. 11:10). Think about how amazing it will be to move into our mansions in heaven and have them fully stocked without having to worry about our budget or lack of funds—*and* everything there will last forever and never have to be replaced! No broken dishes, no tarnished silverware … only the best of the best. Jesus has already paid for it all—we get to just show up and enjoy it.

QUESTION FOR REFLECTION

What practical steps can you take in this life to remind yourself that this dwelling is temporary as you look forward to the city with foundations?

18

MOVING DAY

Therefore keep watch, because you do not know on what day your Lord will come.

MATTHEW 24:42 NIV

During the decade my family and I lived in Cape Town, we spent a year living in the furnished home of some missionaries who went on furlough. Our family had the privilege of looking after their dogs and belongings while they were away. Prior to this twelve-month arrangement, we had spent four months in a different rental nearby.

Shortly after we moved in, my husband's back started to give him problems, so we decided to try a mattress with firmer springs. The day the new mattress was to be delivered, my husband and I hauled the old one out of the master bedroom. Our four-year-old son was lying on the floor playing with Matchbox cars as we passed through the dining room toward the garage. As he saw the mattress floating by, he asked nonchalantly, "Are we moving again today, Mom?"

He wasn't even fazed. We had moved so many times in his short life, apparently it seemed like a normal and natural thing to do on any given day of the week. In many ways, moving so frequently became a blessing because it helped me realize afresh that this is not our home. Since the roots of our earthly dwellings did not grow deep, it became (somewhat) easier to remember that this life is temporary.

Like my son, we should be daily asking our heavenly Father, "Are we moving today, Dad? Is today the day you're going to take me home? Is today the day your Son is coming back?"

When my South African husband was in the process of applying for his US citizenship, there were multiple steps in the process, including an in-person interview and a swearing-in ceremony on separate days, both in a city three hours away from where we lived. The problem was, we didn't know when either of those events would take place. We were told we would receive a letter in the mail notifying us as to when he should show up, but we might only have a week's notice in advance.

My husband wanted to travel to Cape Town to help his mom at one point during the waiting period, but he decided against scheduling a trip, saying, "What if the letter comes while I'm gone and it says I have to be in Detroit sooner than I would be able to make it back to Michigan?" Because he didn't know the day or time he would be expected to show up, he had to be ready at all times.

In Matthew 25:1-13, we read the parable of the ten virgins who took lamps to go wait for the bridegroom. Five of them were foolish and did not take oil for their lamps; the other five were wise and did take oil along. None of them had any idea how long they would have to wait. When the bridegroom finally arrived—much later than anticipated—the virgins who did not take oil realized they were about to run out. They weren't ready. They had to leave to buy more oil, and by the time they returned, they had missed their opportunity to meet the bridegroom. Can you imagine anything more tragic?

In a similar way, we don't know when the Lord will call us into His presence. "Therefore keep watch, because you do not know on what day your Lord will come" (Matt. 24:42 NIV). Will today be the day we get to move to our eternal home? What can we do now to prepare for His coming? May He teach us how to stay ready, covered by the solid and secure promise of His grace.

QUESTION FOR REFLECTION

If Christ returned tomorrow,
would you be ready? If not, why not?

19

STRANGERS IN A FOREIGN LAND

All these people were still living by faith when they died. They did not receive the things promised; they only saw them and welcomed them from a distance, admitting that they were foreigners and strangers on earth. People who say such things show that they are looking for a country of their own. If they had been thinking of the country they had left, they would have had opportunity to return. Instead, they were longing for a better country—a heavenly one.

HEBREWS 11:13-16 NIV

When I stepped onto the plane for my first-ever flight to the African continent, I had no idea just how much things would change. I was saying goodbye to the only town I'd ever known—a predominantly Dutch, middle-class, American suburb—and walking into the bustling, diverse metropolis of Cape Town.

Forget trying to fit in ... the moment I opened my mouth, my tongue betrayed me, and my twangy American accent stuck out like a sore thumb.

The irony is that after spending over ten years dipping Ouma rusks into Rooibos and boerewors into chutney and chakalaka amongst South Africans, the harshness of my American accent was sanded down, and what remains has often not been recognizable to those in my own hometown.

Upon our family's arrival to the States in 2013, people would strike up a conversation with me, and after a few minutes pose the question, "Where are you from?"

I'm from here! I wanted to insist. *Really, I am! It might not sound like it, but I'm one of you!*

If you've ever lived in a foreign context for any length of time, you know what I mean. Maybe it wasn't your accent that changed, but I'm quite confident that some part of you did. Not only that, but the place you left behind changed in your absence, too.

In South Africa, I did my best to make our house a home—and yet even after ten years, the myriad of cultures were still foreign to me. I loved it there—and yet I didn't quite belong. Moving back "home" made me realize I don't quite belong in the States, either.

This is what it's like to live in the in-between. As long as we're between the fall and glory, between creation and the final redemption, we'll never *really* feel as though we belong.

And we're not supposed to.

> We pilgrims walk the tightrope between earth and heaven, feeling trapped in time, yet with eternity beating in our hearts. Our unsatisfied sense of exile is not to be solved or fixed while here on earth. Our

> pain and longings make sure we will never be content, but that's good: it is to our benefit that we do not grow comfortable in a world destined for decay.[28]

We're called to be *in* the world, but not *of* it (John 15:19). We're sojourners on this earth, wanderers, not really fitting in until Christ returns and we will be welcomed into His eternal fold forever.

E. M. Bounds echoes the sentiment that it is good to be "out of sync" with the world:

> Heaven ought to draw and engage us. Heaven ought to so fill our hearts and hands, our manner and our conversation, our character and our features, that all would see that we are foreigners, strangers to this world, natives of a nobler clime, fairer than this. Out of tune, out of harmony, out of course, we must be with this world. The very atmosphere of the world should be chilling to us and noxious, its suns eclipsed and its companionship dull and insipid. Heaven is our native land and home to us, and death to us is not the dying hour, but the birth hour. Heaven should kindle desire, and like a magnet draw us upward to the skies. Duty, inexorable duty, fealty to God, alone, should hold us here.[29]

If you're a believer in the Lord Jesus Christ and yet, in the day-to-day grind of life, you feel that you don't belong—don't fret. *You're not supposed to.* Be glad when your Christian accent clashes with the voices of the world and count it a privilege to belong to Him alone.

QUESTION FOR REFLECTION

In what ways have you felt like a stranger in this world?

20

WHERE ARE YOU FROM?

By the sweat of your face you shall eat bread, till you return to the ground, for out of it you were taken; for you are dust, and to dust you shall return.

GENESIS 3:19

After living in America for five years with our kids who were then ten, twelve, and fifteen, we took a trip to visit South Africa—the land of their birth and the first five to ten years of their upbringing. While visiting a tourist destination in Cape Town, a local asked my kids, "Where are you from?" One of them blurted out, "AMERICA!" The other one said they were from South Africa. The third one paused before replying, "Many places."

I wonder if the main character in the 2015 film *Brooklyn* would introduce herself as Eilis from Brooklyn or Eilis from Ireland. I watched her story unfold and saw my own in the reflection of her eyes. *Am I Kate from Michigan or Kate from South Africa?* I was born and raised in the small, Dutch town of Holland, Michigan. At age 21, I moved to Cape Town, South Africa. What I thought would be a six-month stint turned into ten years.

In 1951, Eilis was miserable living with her mother and sister in her small, gossip-filled town in Ireland. Seeing

Eilis's despondency, her sister made arrangements through an Irish priest named Father Flood for Eilis to move to Brooklyn, New York.

As I watched the scene with emigrants gripping the transatlantic ship's railing with one hand and waving farewell with the other, my own hatred of goodbyes caught hard in my throat. Eilis didn't realize it yet, but her life was about to change forever. Home as she knew it would never be the same.

The initial bouts of homesickness are severe. Eilis battles fiercely, but is overcome. When Father Flood takes notice, Eilis admits her intense struggle. He tries to console her: "We need Irish girls in Brooklyn."

Eilis confesses, "I wish I could stop feeling that I want to be an Irish girl in Ireland."

I know the feeling. I spent five years living in Cape Town before I realized I had stopped mentally converting every price in the grocery store from Rand to dollars, every liter of petrol into gallons of gas, every degree Celsius into Fahrenheit. On some days I longed to be an American girl in America, not South Africa.

Father Flood says to Eilis, "All I can say is that it will pass. Homesickness is like all other sicknesses. It'll make you feel wretched, then it'll move on to somebody else."

Gradually, Eilis realizes the priest may be right. She meets a nice Italian boy named Tony, and they start to date. Like Eilis, I met someone while living overseas. Eilis had to learn how to eat spaghetti with a fork and spoon before visiting her Italian boyfriend's family. I had to learn how to eat mealie pap and tamati gravy with my fingers while visiting my Motswana boyfriend's house. Each in our own way, we formed a new definition of home.

In the film, Eilis receives the tragic news that her sister, Rose, died unexpectedly in Ireland. Upon hearing this, Tony presumes aloud, "You want to go home, I guess?"

Lifting her head from Tony's shoulder, Eilis looks up at him and asks, "How would it be for you if I did go back home?"

He answers, "I'd be afraid every single day."

"Afraid that I wouldn't come back?"

"Yeah. Home is home."

And then the ball drops as Eilis admits: "I'm not sure I have a home anymore."

Eilis does go back to Ireland, but not before Tony persuades her to secretly marry him in a civil court ceremony just before her departure in hopes that their union will secure her return to him.

Back in Ireland, Eilis wrestles again with her identity, her place, her sense of home. The pull is strong. Can she turn her back on such a significant part of her heart? Either choice is a loss. Either choice is gain.

In the end, she packs her bag for the long journey back to New York. On the boat returning to America, another Irish girl learns that this was not Eilis' first voyage and asks, "What's it like in America? I'm going to live in Brooklyn, New York. Do you know it?"

Eilis nods.

The girl prods further. "People say there are so many

Irish people there, it's like home. Is that right?"

Eilis pauses, then answers, "Yes. It's just like home."[30]

For various reasons, we may struggle to answer the question, "Where are you from?" But as believers, the most important answer is that we know with confidence where we are going. And it will be even better than feeling as if it's "just like home."

QUESTION FOR REFLECTION

When have you wrestled with a sense of identity based on where you're from, and how can the promise of eternity help you with those wrestlings?

21

RENOVATIONS

And we all, with unveiled face, beholding the glory of the Lord, are being transformed into the same image from one degree of glory to another.

2 CORINTHIANS 3:18

I love a good "before and after." It doesn't matter if it's laundry, yard work, a cleaning project, or a haircut, I love to compare photographs of something in a less-than-ideal state with the "finished" product after a transformation has taken place.

The first home my husband and I purchased was a fixer-upper. It was built in the 1970s, and very few improvements had been made by previous owners over the decades. When we moved in, we had a *long* list of tasks to complete. We tore out carpet, laid new floors, painted almost every single wall and door, changed the hardware on the doors, added a bedroom and offices to the basement, and more.

After the first few months of hard work, our neighbors asked us how things were going. "We're making progress, but we still have a long list of things to do," my husband answered.

"We've lived here for thirty years," our neighbor said.

"We spent the first twenty years making improvements to our house, and when we finally finished, the first changes we made were twenty years old and we had to start all over again!"

In a similar way, there will always be work to be done in ourselves. At the point of a person's regeneration and conversion, the Holy Spirit moves into the new believer's heart. Full and complete occupation takes place. Sanctification, however, is a gradual and lifelong process. While there is sometimes a radical, immediate change in the life of a young convert, there is still much work to be done. God graciously works on us, room by room, conforming us more and more over time into the likeness of His Son.

Shortly after we moved into our first home, I created two photo albums on my phone: "House Before" and "House After." Years later, I still like looking back on the "Before" pictures and seeing how far we've come and how much better the house looks now than it did when we first bought it.

While it may not be helpful to dwell on past sins, I do think it's helpful for us to look back and remember what we used to be like. The Bible says we were "by nature children of wrath" (Eph. 2:3), "separated from Christ, alienated from the commonwealth of Israel and strangers to the covenants of promise, having no hope and without God in the world" (Eph. 2:12). When I think about how wretched I was (and still would be) apart from grace, the depth of my gratitude for God's rescue is magnified, and my desire to be perfected in eternity increases.

As long as we are in these temporary, fallen bodies, there will always be more work to be done. There will always be areas in which we can grow, improve, and be sanctified. Part of God's plan is to conform us to the image of His Son, Jesus Christ (Rom. 8:29). But the Scriptures make it clear that we don't seek to become better people to earn God's favor or salvation. It doesn't work that way. There's nothing we can do to make God love us more—or less.

Hebrews 10:14 says, "For by a single offering he has perfected for all time those who are being sanctified." According to an article on Crossway.org,

> Perfected for all time does not mean that believers are now already sinless, but that Christ has fully earned their perfection, which will certainly be applied to Christians in God's good time. The eternal perfection (see Heb. 11:40; Heb. 12:23) of the saints stems from the once-for-all-nature of Jesus' sacrifice. Hence, believers look to Christ and not to themselves for a cleansed conscience, full forgiveness of sins, and total flawlessness in the future.[31]

It's a mystery, for sure. The Father looks at us and sees the perfect sacrifice of His Son—and yet as long as we are in these earthly bodies, we continue to chip away at our long list of renovations—until Christ comes again—as a testimony of His goodness to us and our gratitude to Him.

Soon and very soon, our Maker will return, and our bodies will be renewed and made perfect. One glorious day, we will be presented to Christ "as a radiant church, without stain or wrinkle or any other blemish, but holy and blameless" (Eph. 5:27 NIV). Come, Lord Jesus.

QUESTION FOR REFLECTION

In what areas of your life do you still need to be sanctified? How does this realization increase your longing for eternity with God?

22

SURPRISES IN SPRING

Instead of the thornbush will grow the juniper, and instead of briers the myrtle will grow. This will be for the Lord's renown, for an everlasting sign, that will endure forever.

ISAIAH 55:13 NIV

My husband and I lived in various rental homes for the first sixteen years of our marriage. When we finally bought our first home together in Michigan, we moved into the house in late November. If you've ever been to West Michigan in late November, you'll know that there's not much life happening there. Everything on our new property looked dead and brown.

We only met one of our many neighbors because it was too cold and unpleasant for anyone else to venture outside. Everyone just used their remote controls to open their automated garage doors, drove their cars into their garages after work, and closed the doors without being seen. That Christmas, all the church services were canceled due to a severe winter storm. In those cold, blustery months we spent a lot of time working on the interior of our new home but rarely spent time outside, except to shovel mounds of accumulated snow from the driveway.

Eventually, the temperatures started to climb and the snow melted. As the calendar turned toward March and April, signs of life began to emerge. I audibly gasped when I saw the first shoots of green spring forth from the dark earth. We knew the previous homeowner had enjoyed gardening, but we had no idea which flowers or bushes she had planted around the property. We later discovered that she had intentionally spread out the timing of her numerous perennials so something new and different would bloom almost every week.

That first spring in our new home I acted like a giddy schoolgirl, wandering around the yard on our corner lot, watching as each new area of landscaping revealed itself. Every plant that bloomed was a glorious surprise. I had no clue what to expect.

My sister came for a visit one day and pointed to a cluster of small bushes with dark green leaves at the front of our house. "I'm pretty sure those are peonies," she announced. "What?!" I exclaimed. Peonies were my absolute favorites, but I had only ever seen them after they had been picked; I never knew what the bushes or leaves looked like. We looked up a picture online, and the results matched the plants before us. I could hardly contain my excitement. I had inherited my very own peony bushes! When that brief week in June arrived when the buds appeared and slowly opened into the most amazing flourishes of pink and fuchsia, I took photo after photo to preserve the beauty and memory.

At the back of our house, visible from the sliding glass

door, grew another personal treasure: a gorgeous hydrangea in my favorite deep periwinkle color. I love those flowers so much we used them as the centerpieces for our wedding.

My husband teased me that first year as I expressed endless enthusiasm over each new find. We had done nothing to make these plants and flowers appear, and yet they had become ours to behold and enjoy.

As the weather warmed, our neighbors began to emerge as well, and we discovered that we lived next to the sweetest people—kind, generous neighbors who would eventually mow our yard, plow our driveway, lend us mole traps and shovels and wheelbarrows, teach us how to freeze corn, and bless us with bags of homegrown tomatoes in the summer.

I can't help but wonder if the experience I've enjoyed by moving to a new home has been a shadowy glimpse of what it will feel like to arrive at my new home in heaven. Like spring in West Michigan, I imagine that a new delightful surprise will be around every corner, and I will hardly be able to take it all in.

QUESTION FOR REFLECTION

When have you experienced a joyous blessing that you were not expecting, and how might that remind you of the coming surprises in eternity?

23

READY OR NOT

Therefore you also must be ready,
for the Son of Man is coming at
an hour you do not expect.

MATTHEW 24:44

After my husband, kids, and I had been living in the States for eleven years, my husband's South African mother and brother finally had an opportunity to visit us in Michigan. Neither of them had ever been to America before. They would stay with us for four months, and to say I was ecstatic about their visit would be a gross understatement. I started counting days from the moment they received their visas.

We purchased new mattresses, wardrobes, pillows—even a clock with a radio so my mother-in-law could listen to music and the news from her bedroom as she was accustomed to doing every night. We added hooks to the bathroom wall so they could hang their towels and a rack with hangers in the spare bedroom so they could hang their clothes. I even painted an entire wall in our living room, complete with a fireplace and mantel, to make it look more welcoming and presentable.

As the day of their arrival drew nearer, I stocked our

freezer with foods I thought they would like—I bought extra packs of bacon when it was on sale and more chicken wings, bread, cayenne pepper, and lemon juice than we had ever consumed before.

And then the cleaning frenzy began. I scrubbed the shower and tub, swept and mopped the floors, vacuumed the carpet, and wiped the baseboards. I tidied the kitchen cupboards and straightened the bedding in the linen closet. I even got out the heavy-duty carpet cleaning machine that my husband bought for rare deep-cleaning occasions—as this was one such occasion! The day before their flight was due to land, I hired my friend who cleans houses for a living to help me with a final polish. I wanted the whole place to look better than ever.

Imagine if they had changed their flights without telling me and arrived a week before I expected them. Although I still would have been thrilled to see them, I would have been embarrassed by the state of my home. They would have found drop cloths draped across living room furniture, wet paintbrushes, and open paint cans. Beds would not have been made, and the refrigerator might have been empty.

As much as I said I would never be the type of person who rushes around to clean their house as soon as they hear visitors are coming over, that is the woman I have become. Never ready without advance notice. And yet "ready" is exactly what I'm supposed to be when it comes to the most important visitor I could ever anticipate.

While I rarely wake up and think about the second

coming of Christ, we're told in the Scriptures that it could happen any day. Not even Jesus knows the exact time: "But about that day or hour no one knows, not even the angels in heaven, nor the Son, but only the Father" (Matt. 24:36 NIV).

As I was rushing around like a madwoman trying to get my house ready to welcome my mother-in-law and brother-in-law for the very first time, the Lord convicted me about how much effort and time I was putting into my preparations for their arrival, and how little time I had spent thinking about His upcoming arrival. While it wasn't wrong for me to want to be hospitable or to give them a pleasant experience in America, I spent a disproportionate amount of mental and physical energy getting ready for their visit compared to my preparations for the return of Christ. My excitement level for their cross-continental trip was through the roof. I was telling everyone who crossed my path: "My family is coming! They've never been here before! They're staying for four months!" I could hardly sleep, I was so ecstatic. Can I say the same about my excitement and anticipation for Jesus' return?

May the Lord increase our eagerness for His arrival, and may we be ever ready for His return.

QUESTION FOR REFLECTION

What do you need to do to prepare your heart for Christ's arrival?

24

PLANTING SWEETS

Do not be deceived: God cannot be mocked. A man reaps what he sows. Whoever sows to please their flesh, from the flesh will reap destruction; whoever sows to please the Spirit, from the Spirit will reap eternal life.

GALATIANS 6:7-8 NIV

One spring morning after church, a friend gave our four-year-old daughter a piece of candy. She cupped it in her palm, then wrapped her toddler fingers around it as if it were more precious than gold. Her fist tightly clasped, she could barely contain her glee as she skipped around the church parking lot clutching her newly acquired treasure.

About half an hour later, I noticed that her hands were empty.

"Where did your sweet go?" I asked her.

"Oh, I planted it over there," she explained nonchalantly, "so it will grow into a tree full of sweets."

I smiled at her logic. At the age of four, she already understood the concept of reaping what you sow. What you put in is what you get out. As my daughter reasoned, if you put something good into the soil, something good will come out of it. Sadly, the converse is also true. When we allow our minds to be flooded with the things of this world, we will no doubt be negatively influenced and affected.

As we can see in the verses quoted above, according to the apostle Paul, what we sow into our lives can and will have lasting effects—for good or for bad.

We're not just talking about a minor repercussion here or there, or a temporary perk or benefit. The Bible says the decisions we make now could have eternal consequences. We're talking about destruction versus eternal life.

In her Bible study material for the book of Genesis, Jen Wilkin considers the story when Esau comes in from the field and begs his twin brother Jacob for some stew (Gen. 25:29-30). Jacob convinces Esau to sell his birthright to Jacob in exchange for a portion of stew (Gen. 25:31-34). For context, "The birthright was what entitled the oldest son to a double portion of the inheritance." She continues:

> Esau sacrificed the permanent on the altar of the temporary. ... Sacrificing the permanent on the altar of the temporary can look many ways for us, but I think we can look at Esau and not be too hard on him, knowing that we ourselves have done similar things. That we too can sometimes despise our birthright as the children of God, taking lightly the gift of relationship with Him, the gift of having His Word daily at our disposal. When we treat these things lightly and we're more concerned with matters of,

> as Jesus would say, what we will eat or what we will wear, then what have we done? We have stored up treasure for ourself in the temporary rather than focused on the eternal, the permanent.[32]

Instead, we should be thinking about how we can give up the temporary—recognizing it for what it really is—in favor of storing up treasure in heaven. Like my preschool daughter's decision to plant her sweet in hopes of a future bounty, we should take what we prize and value most—the gospel of Jesus Christ—and plant it in fertile soil with great anticipation and expectation.

If we take what is precious and bury it where it will reap an eternal harvest, we will have not only a tree, but fields ripe and plentiful. So let's seek to find the richest of soil and dig deep. Plant your treasure where the rain falls gently all around, and when the shoot springs up, may it be strong and confident like the sunflower, with its face always turned toward the sun.

QUESTION FOR REFLECTION

What treasure have you planted, and what harvest are you expecting will be reaped from your sowing?

25

WHEN HOME HURTS

For you are my rock and my fortress;
and for your name's sake you lead me and
guide me; you take me out of the net they
have hidden for me, for you are my refuge.

PSALM 31:3-4

It's the child who lingers as long as possible on the school grounds after the building has been locked, shuffling feet and kicking pebbles, unwilling to leave, for fear of what he might find at home.

It's the single mom who got the final foreclosure letter from the bank in the mail and has nowhere else to turn.

It's the husband who stays late at the office every night then heads to the bar for drinks to numb the pain and diminish the number of hours he has to listen to his nagging wife and whining kids when he eventually drags himself home.

It's the widow suffocating from the tight grip of empty space, who cries silent tears into the screaming void of a lonely house.

For far too many, home hurts.

The bad news is, it will always hurt on this side of eternity. For those in situations where home hurts, where home is a place to be avoided at all costs … heaven might not be all that appealing. In fact, the very thought of being trapped in a home forever might sound downright appalling.

Almost every visit I made to the States during the ten years I lived in South Africa was motivated by my mom's terminal illness. While I was always grateful for the opportunity, a nagging fear remained in the pit of my stomach, like a hungry dog gnawing on a bone. I never knew what I would find on the other side of the ocean.

Often, it hurt.

It was wonderful and sometimes unbearably painful all at once. I wanted to be there and I wanted to run away, all at the same time. I wanted to capture the frames and freeze them into a still life, and I wanted to blot them with black ink so they would never be seen again.

One stanza from the poem "Home," by Edgar Guest, reminds me that sometimes the aching spots are the most tender spots, and may one day even morph into endearing memories:

Ye've got t' weep t' make it home,
  ye've got t' sit an' sigh
An' watch beside a loved one's bed,
  an' know that Death is nigh;
An' in the stillness o' the night t'
  see Death's angel come,
An' close the eyes o' her that smiled,
  an' leave her sweet voice dumb.

Fer these are scenes that grip the heart,
an' when yer tears are dried,
Ye find the home is dearer than it was,
an' sanctified;
An' tuggin' at ye always are the pleasant memories
O' her that was an' is no more—
ye can't escape from these.[33]

While we "can't escape from these" "scenes that grip the heart," sometimes we find that "home is dearer than it was, an' sanctified." The word *sanctified* sounds like an intruder in these scenes that grip the heart—scenes that etch and engrave themselves with sharp, pointed tips and leave scars on our insides. But the apostle Peter tells us that the word *sanctified* is neither imposter nor traitor here: "Though now for a little while you may have had to suffer grief in all kinds of trials. These have come so that the proven genuineness of your faith—of greater worth than gold, which perishes even though refined by fire—may result in praise, glory and honor when Jesus Christ is revealed" (1 Pet. 1:6-7 NIV).

The apostle Paul echoes these sentiments that suffering is not in vain, for "suffering produces endurance, and endurance produces character, and character produces hope" (Rom. 5:3-4). So take heart, even when home hurts, for there is purpose in your pain. Though we fumble and stumble our way down the driveway, bruised and wounded and groaning with all of creation, the promise remains: the Owner of the mansion stands on the doorstep, holding out the key to your room. For those who have been granted the grace to have faith in the One who paid for it all, a perfect, pain-free room is waiting with your name chiseled into the door.

QUESTION FOR REFLECTION

If home has had painful aspects for you, how does the anticipation of eternity with the Lord give you hope?

26

UPSIDE-DOWN CHOICES

You will be hated by everyone because of me,
but the one who stands firm to the end will be saved.

MATTHEW 10:22 NIV

In the book of Acts, the apostle Paul "sent to Ephesus and called the elders of the church to come to him" so he could bid them farewell (Acts 20:17). In part of his address to them, he said, "I am going to Jerusalem, constrained by the Spirit, not knowing what will happen to me there, except that the Holy Spirit testifies to me in every city that imprisonment and afflictions await me. But I do not account my life of any value nor as precious to myself, if only I may finish my course and the ministry that I received from the Lord Jesus, to testify to the gospel of the grace of God" (Acts 20:22-24). Paul had a single-minded goal: to be faithful to the Lord's calling on his life.

He had no idea what would happen to him when he reached Jerusalem, but it was probably not going to be pleasant. And yet he set his face toward the destination God had called him to, knowing he would likely face significant hardships and trials.

Pastor Andrew Davis points out that often believers

are called to forfeit earthly pleasures and accept temporary pain and heartache, with the anchor of faith holding the boat of hope firmly to the seabed, grounded in the promises of God's Word. In his chapter on "Will—What You Choose and What You Reject," Davis writes,

> A spiritually mature person, like Jesus, accepts that pain and suffering are an intrinsic part of this sin-cursed world, but that ultimate pleasure still exists and can be ours. However, by faith we accept that ultimate pleasure can be ours only in one place: in the New Heaven and the New Earth, at the completion of God's redemptive plan. By faith we accept that forward-looking stance, as we have already mentioned. Then we choose to do what is **not** apparently in our own immediate best interests, even to the loss of every single earthly advantage and to the "gaining" of much earthly pain. We choose to *"deny ourselves, take up our cross daily and follow Christ"* (Matthew 16:24). We choose this, though it seems utterly foolish to unbelievers. We choose this, because we are really choosing infinitely greater and more lasting pleasure in the next age.[34]

I recently studied the book of Ephesians with some women at my church using Bible study material by Jackie Hill Perry, Jasmine Holmes, and Melissa Kruger. We talked about the fact that Paul was imprisoned at the time he wrote his letter to the Ephesians (Eph. 3:1; 4:1), and yet his words and prayers overflow with praise and rejoicing over the abundant spiritual blessings he possesses in Christ. Not once do we read about him asking the Lord to "please get me out of jail." That would definitely be at the top of my prayer list if I were in his situation!

But as the writers of the Ephesians study pointed out, "Because Paul's eternal future was secure, he knew his hardships were temporary. He might have been in prison then, but one day, he would be in glory! Future hope gives us present joy, even when our circumstances are difficult and painful."[35]

I imagine there were times in Paul's life when the verse quoted at the beginning of this entry felt true—that he was hated by everyone because of Christ. And yet the Lord gave him the grace and strength to stand firm to the end. May He do the same for us, for His glory.

QUESTION FOR REFLECTION

Describe some situations when you were ridiculed, teased, or mocked for trusting in Christ. How did the Lord sustain your faith during those times?

27

WHEN YOU DON'T WANT TO GO HOME

Better is one day in your courts than a thousand elsewhere.

PSALM 84:10 NIV

On one of the first occasions my African-born children ever experienced the exhilarating rush of a sledding hill, my seven-year-old daughter let the adrenaline get to her head. In a moment of boldness, she dove headfirst onto her circular plastic disc, soared down the snow-covered hill, and biffed, chin skidding across the ice. A howl could be heard from the bottom of the hill to the top, and the best I could do was to dab her bloody chin with a used tissue. Over the decibels of her wailing, I asked, "Do you want to go home?"

"Nooo!" she exclaimed adamantly between sobs.

Of course she didn't want to go home. Why would she? In comparison to a perfect (albeit slightly bloodied) sledding hill, home was a dull and boring second-class pick.

If you're a parent, it's quite likely that when you've gone to fetch your kids from a playdate at a friend's house, you've been welcomed with the infamous whine: "I don't wanna go home!"

While home is meant to be a place of comfort and

refuge, there are plenty of places that we think are nicer than home. Don't we sometimes have the same view of heaven, in comparison to the pleasures on earth?

If given the chance, many of us would be hesitant to relinquish what we have here in favor of entering the gates of glory. We can't imagine leaving our beloved families behind. We grasp desperately to our property and occupations, grieving the imminent loss of all we've strived to achieve.

This kind of thinking indicates two problems: First, it reveals the form of our idols. An idol is anything that we desire more than God. What have you elevated in your heart above your desire to be in God's presence?

Second, gripping frantically to our lives here on earth and all that this world has to offer indicates a warped view of heaven. When we think this world is too good to leave, clearly we haven't caught the vision for what heaven will be like.

Many believers in the church today aren't excited about heaven and can think of no good reason to look forward to it. It's common to imagine endless years of sitting on a cloud, strumming a golden harp … and how boring would *that* be?[36]

In his book *Mere Christianity*, C. S. Lewis gives this diagnosis: "Most of us find it very difficult to want 'Heaven' at all—except in so far as 'Heaven' means meeting again our friends who have died. One reason for this difficulty is that we have not been trained: our whole education tends to fix our minds on this world."[37]

If, somehow, you found out that you were about to die, what is the first lament that would come to your mind? Would you be sad to lose the wealth you've labored so hard to build? Would you immediately mourn over the separation from loved ones? It's certainly not wrong to grieve over an imminent separation from those we love. God has made us to live in community. The danger occurs when the desire to stay far exceeds the desire to be with God. Though it can be difficult to think this way, the apostle Paul says it is better to depart and be with Christ (Phil. 1:23).

Kara Tippetts, a young wife and mother, was diagnosed with terminal cancer. During her battle with the disease, she wrote the following words:

> None of us have the strength to loosen our grip, untie the knots, open wide our hands to the loves we love. We lack imagination for life beyond what we can see, feel, smell, and taste. We are reckless in grasping for more time, and forget that the best is yet to come. We simply have so little imagination for our forever home, and yet I feel that Jesus is very gentle with us in our lack of understanding.[38]

If, like my daughter on the sledding hill, you're not eager to go home, ask the Lord to show you how He might change your mindset and understanding. Pray that He would reveal any idols that may be hidden in your heart and give you the grace to dethrone them. As long as we're in these earthly bodies, we will daily struggle with competing desires. May the Lord continue to increase our longing for Himself.

QUESTION FOR REFLECTION

What aspects of your life on earth have you elevated above your desire to be with God?

28

TUG OF WAR

I am torn between the two: I desire to depart and be with Christ, which is better by far; but it is more necessary for you that I remain in the body.

PHILIPPIANS 1:23-24 NIV

A local college in my hometown has an annual tradition called The Pull. It's basically a glorified tug-of-war competition between eighteen students graduating in odd-numbered years, and eighteen who will graduate in even-numbered years. The students train for weeks leading up to the momentous occasion. On the day of the event, a thick rope is stretched across a river, and the opposing teams dig pits on either bank. The starting signal is fired, and The Pull begins. On some occasions, the tug-of-war lasts for hours before a clear victory is determined.

I feel this pull in my own heart. On the one hand, when I look around at all the brokenness in the world, the seemingly endless flow of pain and heartache, I long to escape from it all and experience the unimaginable peace and joy that will be found in God's presence in glory. Yet on the other hand, I love so many things about this incredible life God has given me, and I'm certainly not eager to leave my husband or kids behind.

Imagine if one team competing in The Pull was yanked straight into the river—an obvious defeat—and yet they refused to let go of the rope. Sometimes that's how I act when I think about leaving this world. Instead, I should be thinking this way: "The hope of heaven should fill us with a joy of anticipation that loosens our hearts from this transitory world."[39]

At times we grasp desperately to the rope tying us to this world. John MacArthur points out Paul's description of this feeling in 2 Corinthians 5:6-8.

> There is a tendency for most of us to hold tightly to this world because it is all that we know. It is familiar to us. All our dearest relationships are built here. We too easily think of it as home. So we become captive to this life. But when Paul says he is willing to be "present" with the Lord, he employs the Greek word *endemeo*, which literally means "to be at home." We are most truly "at home" only when we are finally with the Lord. Paul understood this. And the knowledge that he belonged in heaven was the very thing that helped him endure the struggles of this life.[40]

What a blessing to know that once we are present with the Lord, only then, will we truly be "at home." Thank God that His hand is stronger, and He will win the pull for those who are called His own.

Consider the wisdom in this quote by E. M. Bounds:

> Great earthly attachments lessen heavenly attachments. The heart which indulges itself in great earthly loves will have less for heaven. God's great work and often His most afflictive and chastening work is to unfasten our hearts from earth and fasten them to heaven, to break up and desolate the earthly home that we may seek a home in heaven.[41]

When I was in elementary school, I hated the monkey bars on the playground. I was always afraid that if I let go of one bar, I would fall to the ground. But to make it across to the other side, I had to let go of what was in my grasp in order to open my hand for the next bar. If I didn't let go, I would never land on the next platform. In a similar way, when we cling too tightly to the metal bar of our earthly lives, we're unable to open our hands to grip onto what comes next to make it to the other side.

Just like with The Pull, various aspects of this life will continue to pull on the rope of our hearts as they're stretched across the river. But a day is coming when the internal fight will be over. The tug-of-war strands will be cut, the rope of tension will fall slack, and we will land on the banks of His side of the river. On that day, our affections will no longer be pulled in multiple directions; instead, our utmost joy, delight, and hope will be found in Him alone.

QUESTION FOR REFLECTION

Which "earthly attachments" might God be nudging you to release so you can "fasten" your heart to heaven?

29

TOO MANY GOODBYES

And everyone who has left houses or brothers or sisters or father or mother or children or lands, for my name's sake, will receive a hundredfold and will inherit eternal life.

MATTHEW 19:29

I have a love/hate relationship with airports. Okay, mostly hate.

Airports are actually capable of causing my stomach to churn, heave, and threaten to wretch, just by the very sight of them. It's not that I get airsick. I don't. (Well, except for that one time when I reacted horribly to an Ambien on the way to India, but that's a different story.)

No, my stomach doesn't literally betray me due to motion sickness. It's a heartsick thing. There have been far too many goodbyes.

Sure, there have been giddy days of counting hours and minutes and practically climbing on strangers' backs in the arrivals terminal to get that first glimpse through the automatic sliding doors leading to the baggage claim conveyor belts. But in my personal travel experience, even when I'm bubbling over with excitement to go—someone always has to be left behind.

Too many times, I left my family in the States to go

back to my husband and kids in South Africa, not knowing if I would ever see my parents or sister again.

Those are gut-wrenching moments. Moments when the ventricles of my heart engaged in a vicious tug-of-war, with two sides of the Atlantic pulling with all their might, and neither side willing to let go.

In his novel about the Norwegian experience of America entitled *The Emigrants*, Jon Bojer describes this feeling:

> If you came back, you wanted to leave again; if you went away, you longed to come back. Wherever you were, you could hear the call of the homeland, like the note of a herdsman's horn far away in the hills. You had one home out there, and one over here, and yet you were an alien in both places. Your true abiding-place was the vision of something very far off, and your soul was like the waves, always restless, forever in motion.[42]

As noted in the last entry, the apostle Paul felt it too, in a far more spiritual sense. In Philippians 1:23-24 (NIV), he wrote, "I am torn between the two: I desire to depart and be with Christ, which is better by far; but it is more necessary for you that I remain in the body."

I don't want to be torn when it's time to go home. When the intercom announces the final boarding call to that ultimate flight, that passage between this life and the next, I pray that the goodbyes will pale in comparison to the destination that awaits. I want to run forward down the corridor with giddy schoolgirl anticipation, finally able to meet the One waiting at the arrivals gate in glory.

It won't be wrong for me to stand in the departures terminal with tears streaming down my face for all that I have to leave behind. God gives us relationships and possessions here on earth for our enjoyment. But they are temporary. If I'm standing with feet firmly planted on the tacky airport pseudo-carpet, lamenting over the fact that I can't take any luggage with me aboard the aircraft—well, then I have a problem.

John MacArthur explains a possible component to our lack of desire for heaven: "I have actually heard Christians say they don't want to go to heaven until they've enjoyed all that the world can deliver. When all earthly pursuits are exhausted, or when age and sickness hamper their enjoyment, then they believe they'll be ready for heaven. 'Please God, don't take me to heaven yet,' they pray. 'I haven't even been to Hawaii!'"[43]

Clearly if we think Hawaii is better than heaven, our understanding is warped. If we think anything could be better than living in perfect harmony and peace with the God of the universe, free from all suffering, pain, sin, and shame, we haven't understood what eternity with the Lord will be.

QUESTION FOR REFLECTION

Which aspects of this life do you anticipate will be most difficult for you to leave behind? How can you start loosening your grip on those elements of your life now in preparation for the life to come?

30

AVOIDING HOME

For the Son of Man came to seek and to save the lost.

LUKE 19:10

What is it that keeps you from wanting to go home? Is it a lack of knowledge of what it will be like, or a common misconception about eternity? Or is it something else?

In a 2009 film called *Everybody's Fine*, the main character, played by Robert De Niro, is a retired, recently widowed man who is looking forward to gathering his four adult children around one table. However, one by one, they call to cancel, giving some excuse or another for not being able to make it to the family reunion. The truth is, none of them want to go home. De Niro makes up his mind, against his doctor's strict orders, to travel across the United States by plane, train, bus, and taxi to visit each of his children. It's a risky sacrifice for De Niro, who ends up paying for it by experiencing a heart attack and landing in the hospital. As the movie unfolds, it becomes clear that each of the adult children were avoiding the reality of going home because of hidden sin or poor choices in their lives. Yet their father goes to them. He searches for them and seeks them out, even while they are avoiding him and masking their sin and wrongdoing.

Maybe you're avoiding the realities of death, heaven, and hell because of some lurking sin tucked away in the crevices of your heart. Perhaps you think you can avoid going home. Maybe you're dreading it. If that's the case, consider this: God has not traveled by plane, train, or bus across a couple of states to get to you. He left His throne in glory to travel to a dirty stable. He spent years covered in sawdust as a carpenter, sweating and toiling. He carried His own cross and drank the cup of His Father's wrath to make it possible for you to get home.

In the Gospel of Luke, Jesus tells a parable about a woman who lost a precious coin:

> Or what woman, having ten silver coins, if she loses one coin, does not light a lamp and sweep the house and seek diligently until she finds it? And when she has found it, she calls together her friends and neighbors, saying, "Rejoice with me, for I have found the coin that I had lost." Just so, I tell you, there is joy before the angels of God over one sinner who repents. (Luke 15:8-10)

Obviously the coin in this story was not hiding intentionally, but it held great value to the woman. Imagine how much more valuable you are to the One who made you for Himself. Then think about how much more offensive it is to God when we hide on purpose. Yet the Bible offers this unfathomable truth: "While we were still sinners, Christ died for us" (Rom. 5:8). Think about that for a moment. Even when we avoid Him, try to hide or deny our transgressions, or call and leave a message on voicemail because we don't want to go home, He "came to seek and to save the lost" (Luke 19:10). Despite our tainted and rebellious selves, the Lord Jesus continues to pursue us for our good and His glory.

Consider this perspective from Nancy Guthrie:

> Sometimes the difficulties of life, the loneliness of life in this world, are overwhelming, aren't they? We find ourselves just wanting to go home. We're like Paul, we would rather be "away from the body and at home with the Lord." Like Abraham, we are seeking a homeland. …
>
> But don't we have to also admit that there are times when our hearts really aren't set on that home? That sometimes we find ourselves so tied to this world, so enamored by it, so invested in it that we actually yawn at this future promise of being at home with God? Well, the good news of the gospel is that Jesus showed the true zeal for God's house that we often lack. His zeal has been credited to our spiritual account.[44]

A day is coming when God's "desire to dwell with us will have been satisfied, and all that is lacking in our desire to dwell with Him will have been provided to us. Our hearts will have finally caught up to His, so that we will be fully at home in His presence."[45]

No more hiding. No more avoiding. No more pretending. Just fully at home, fully embraced, fully known, fully loved.

QUESTION FOR REFLECTION

In what ways might you be avoiding the Lord or hiding something in your life that does not give Him glory? What steps can you take to get back on His planned path for you and accept His grace and forgiveness?

PACKING SUITCASES

Do not lay up for yourselves treasures on earth, where moth and rust destroy and where thieves break in and steal, but lay up for yourselves treasures in heaven, where neither moth nor rust destroys and where thieves do not break in and steal. For where your treasure is, there your heart will be also.

MATTHEW 6:19-21

Before moving to South Africa, I had never packed my life into two suitcases. What a chore it was to decide which of my possessions were worthy of viewing the sights of Cape Town. I spent hours debating what to pack and what to leave behind. I pored over the decision, then jumped and stomped and laid on my luggage, trying to get its bulging sides to zip closed.

Back then, I was allowed to have two bags weighing fifty pounds each. That's 100 pounds of stuff. Forty-five kilograms of earthly possessions that I thought I couldn't live without for 180 consecutive days. It's embarrassing now, looking back and realizing my ignorance as to my relative richness in comparison to so many in the world. I met people in South Africa who didn't have enough cumulative possessions to fill one suitcase, let alone two.

And there I was, on numerous occasions over the next decade, emotionally torn over having to bid farewell to certain sentimental belongings.

Over time, the Lord has revealed to me just how tightly my heart was entwined around earthly possessions. I can't tell you how many times I had to repent and ask forgiveness from my children for overreacting when something in our home was damaged or broken because of careless or reckless behavior. I'm embarrassed to admit how worked up I could get when things broke.

But then, when my kids were the ones upset over a broken toy, a ripped drawing, or a lost book, I would nonchalantly remind them, "Well … we can't take it to heaven, can we?" It's a lesson I'm still cementing in the wet foundation of my faith. Hoarding treasures and pleasures here on earth is like trying to hoard bubbles in a bath. They will quickly pop and disappear, and we will be left with nothing.

The story is told of an American tourist who visited a nineteenth-century Polish rabbi, Hofetz Chaim. Astonished to see that the rabbi's home was only a simple room filled with books, plus a table and bench, the tourist asked, "Rabbi, where is your furniture?"

"Where is yours?" replied the rabbi.

"Mine?" asked the puzzled American. "But I'm a visitor here. I'm only passing through."

"So am I," said Hofetz Chaim.[46]

Can I say the same of myself? In His famous Sermon on the Mount, Jesus instructs His listeners not to lay up "treasures on earth, where moth and rust destroy and where thieves break in and steal .... For where your treasure is, there your heart will be also" (Matt. 6:19, 21).

Randy Alcorn offers a practical application of this passage:

> By telling us that our hearts follow our treasure, Jesus is saying, "Show me your checkbook, your VISA statement, and your receipts, and I'll show you where your heart is."
>
> Suppose you buy shares of General Motors. What happens? You suddenly develop interest in GM. You check the financial pages. You see a magazine article about GM and read every word, even though a month ago you would have passed right over it.
>
> Suppose you're giving to help African children with AIDS. When you see an article on the subject, you're hooked. If you're sending money to plant churches in India and an earthquake hits India, you watch the news and fervently pray.
>
> As surely as the compass needle follows north, your heart will follow your treasure. Money leads; hearts follow.
>
> I've heard people say, "I want more of a heart for missions." I always respond, "Jesus tells us exactly how to get it. Put your money in missions—and in your church and the poor—and your heart will follow."
>
> Do you wish you cared more about eternal things? Then reallocate some of your money, maybe *most* of

your money, from temporal things to eternal things. Watch what happens.[47]

What about you? Do you become irrationally upset when your material possessions are broken or lost? If so, what does that say about where your treasure has been stored?

QUESTION FOR REFLECTION

Are you living your life as a visitor here,
as though you're only passing through?
Or have you planted your stakes firm and deep
in the love and convictions of this world?

LOST PROPERTY

For we know that if the tent that is our earthly home is destroyed, we have a building from God, a house not made with hands, eternal in the heavens.

2 CORINTHIANS 5:1

In 2011, friends of ours arrived home one afternoon to discover that their apartment was on fire. The damage was so extensive that the building had to be torn down. Our friends had no choice but to find somewhere else to live. With two young boys, they were left depending on the donations of others to clothe them until they could claim insurance for the damages.

During the whole ordeal, the strength of their faith was a powerful testimony. The peace of Christ radiated from them as they gave thanks and praise to the Lord for His grace in sparing their lives. They quickly realized that while the possessions in their burned-down apartment were important and valuable to them, they were not everything.

In September 2024, a hurricane ripped through the southeastern United States, ravaging property and devastating lives throughout multiple states. Amanda Held Opelt reflected afterward, "When Hurricane Helene tore through Southern Appalachia, every stream, every tributary, and every underground spring in the mountains became a raging torrent. Our beloved waters that made this place home suddenly took so many homes away."[48]

How should we, as Christians, respond when possessions as monumental as family homes are snatched away or lost to external circumstances?

Opelt went on to observe, "This feeling of the absence of home in the wake of a disaster is perhaps a gift, a way of knowing that deep in our hearts we long for sacred belonging, and what we long for will be given to us someday."[49]

Decades ago, one missionary told the story of a new convert in India who went to church week after week in tattered clothes that were torn and disintegrating. When the missionary offered to help, the woman explained that she used to be wealthy, but heathens had robbed her of her jewels and estate. The heathens promised to give everything back if she would renounce Jesus Christ. In that moment, the woman resolved, "I would rather be a poor Christian than a wealthy heathen."[50]

The writer of the book of Hebrews speaks of those who "joyfully accepted the confiscation of your property, because you knew that you yourselves had better and lasting possessions" (Heb. 10:34 NIV). What about you? Would you willingly sacrifice riches in this life—even something as significant as your home—for the promise of lasting, eternal riches in the life to come? Would you "joyfully accept the confiscation of your property" because of a deep conviction of future inheritance?

We can delight in the assurance that "because our home in Heaven will never burn, flood, or be blown away, we'll never have to wonder whether home will still be there when we return. The new heavens and new earth will never disappear. They'll give a wonderful permanence to the word *home*."[51] The Bible says we can expect "an inheritance that is imperishable, undefiled, and unfading, kept in heaven for you" (1 Pet. 1:4). As Randy Alcorn reminds us, "And that is exactly what God promises us—a home that will not be destroyed, a kingdom that will not fade, a city with unshakable foundations, an incorruptible inheritance."[52]

One day we won't have to fear the loss or destruction of our property, because it will be indestructible and immovable, guarded and preserved by the Lord Himself.

QUESTION FOR REFLECTION

When have you mourned the loss of a material possession? How does the hope of heaven give you a fresh perspective on that loss?

33

CRAVING HOME

As the deer pants for streams of water,
so my soul pants for you, my God.

PSALM 42:1 NIV

For me, sixth grade was hands down the worst school year of my entire educational career. It was my first year of middle school, in a new building that combined students from multiple elementary schools in the district. I didn't know anyone in my class, and I struggle to make friends. To make matters worse, we were required to go to sixth grade camp for a week.

As a homebody who didn't like sleeping other places —especially without any family or friends nearby—I dreaded each day leading up to the week of camp. I even asked my teachers if there was a way I could be excused. They said no. I considered faking an illness, but figured my mom would see through the charade. When I got there, I was miserable. I cried. I begged to go home. As I shared in my memoir, *A Place to Land,*

> Even though my teachers wouldn't let me go home, they did offer a compromise: they allowed my mom to come to the campsite for a night. So my selfless

mother drove to the campgrounds after work one day and slept on the floor of the cabin, amidst a slew of bunk beds and smelly sixth graders. She woke up before the sun the next morning and drove the long distance home to be at work in time. She couldn't grant me my heart's desire to go home, but she could grant me the gift of her presence. And that night, that was enough.[53]

Sometimes we ask things of God—we may even cry and beg and plead, and still His answer may be "no" or "not yet."

Maybe you're suffering from a debilitating disease, and you're ready to go to your true home. You've had enough of this world. You've told God you're ready, but still you open your eyes each morning to the same aches and pains and monotonous routine as yesterday.

He might not let us go home when we want to—but He does send us His Spirit to lay on the floor next to the bunk bed in our darkest of nights.

In *Mere Christianity*, C. S. Lewis writes:

> Most people, if they had really learned to look into their own hearts, would know that they do want, and want acutely, something that cannot be had in this world. There are all sorts of things in this world that offer to give it to you, but they never quite keep their promise. The longings which arise in us when we first fall in love, or first think of some foreign

country, or first take up some subject that excites us, are longings which no marriage, no travel, no learning, can really satisfy.[54]

The first stanza of a hymn by Johann Meyfart eloquently articulates this longing:

Jerusalem, whose towers touch the skies,
  I yearn to come to you!
Your shining streets have drawn my longing eyes
  My lifelong journey through.
And though I roam the woodland,
  The city, and the plain,
My heart still seeks the good land,
  My Father's house to gain.[55]

My Father's house to gain. When I was in sixth grade, I thought it was my own home that I wanted. I didn't know then that even the comfort and familiarity of my earthly home could not fully satisfy my longings. Only my Father's house can do that.

In His sovereignty, the Lord may not answer our prayers exactly as we hope—but He always, *always* grants us the gift of His presence.

And while we wait for the call to join Him in glory, that is enough.

QUESTION FOR REFLECTION

Which home are you craving most,
and how has God blessed you with an
awareness of His presence here and now?

34

THIS IS NOT OUR HOME

Now the LORD said to Abram,
"Go from your country and your
kindred and your father's house to
the land that I will show you."

GENESIS 12:1

One morning I flipped the page on my DaySpring desk calendar and found the following quote by Heather Gemmen Wilson: "I don't plan to ever get comfortable enough in this world that I forget about the real one."

I liked it so much that I cut it out and stuck it on my fridge as a visual reminder. And yet, I confess that when I moved back to the United States after living in South Africa for ten years, I quickly and effortlessly slipped back into the many comforts and conveniences of America. Drive-thru banking, drive-thru car washes, drive-thru pharmacies, online grocery pickup orders, two-day Amazon deliveries. It has been *very* easy to get so comfortable in this world that I forget about the real one.

In 2024, some friends of mine made the drastic decision to pack up their family of eight (including six kids aged twelve and under) and move from the east coast of South Africa to the west coast of Namibia for eighteen months. They thought it would be a bit of a family adventure, a change from the regular work routine, and a way to break out of the "bubble" of their hometown and expose their kids to a different part of the world before they started high school and moved out of the house for college. While the family enjoyed their new culture and surroundings, my friend also admitted, "The kids miss home a lot, but it's good that they struggle a bit. It's easy to parent when things are comfortable and good."

By intentionally moving to an environment that included aspects of discomfort, these parents opened a door for their kids (and themselves) to grow in their understanding of longing for a better place to come. While this tactic may not be feasible for every family, it is certainly one way to create a daily, tangible reminder that this world is not our home. It's temporary. It's broken.

> Wherever we find ourselves, our earthly homes fail all of us. …
>
> Home isn't always a refuge. We pine for marriage and stay single. We want children and birth barrenness. At our tables too many of us find loneliness instead of company. And immune though we may be in North America from the domestic ravages of war and famine, we watch as home's broken promises wash up on beaches facedown. None of us, not even those of us in middle-class America, can be persuaded that this is the best of all possible worlds. …
>
> But perhaps our common grief—of crossing

> borders, mourning death, lamenting strained relationships, and generally feeling earth's ill-fit—is a severe mercy. No doubt it helps us understand that home is not now, not yet. Homelessness teaches us, not least, that something has gone terribly wrong in the world.[56]

Whenever I visit my mom's grave, I step gingerly through the rows of graves and headstones, reading the names, dates, and epitaphs. Every time, my own grief and deep personal loss are overshadowed by sympathy for others. For me, walking through a cemetery is an incredibly humbling ritual. There is nothing quite like it to remind me that this world is most definitely not our home.

In our nearsightedness, it's common to focus on what is right in front of us and forget about what awaits beyond the horizon. And yet with each day, month, and year that passes, I'm reminded that so much of life is a process of letting go of my emotional attachments to the here and now in order to cling to the hope of what lies ahead.

QUESTION FOR REFLECTION

What practical changes can you make in your life to remind yourself regularly that this life is not your true home?

A LITTLE WHILE

And after you have suffered a little while, the God of all grace, who has called you to his eternal glory in Christ, will himself restore, confirm, strengthen, and establish you.

1 PETER 5:10

After my parents got divorced when I was seven years old, my mom, my younger sister, and I moved from a 3,000-square-foot home to a 500-square-foot pump house that had been converted into a two-bedroom rental property. The friends who helped us move stacked boxes of our possessions from floor to ceiling in the one-stall attached garage. We had to walk through the garage to get into the house, which meant we carved out a narrow, winding path between stacks of cardboard boxes and wobbly towers of Rubbermaid storage totes.

Initially, my mom said we would only be staying there for a few months until she found her feet financially. We kept most of our belongings in those boxes in the garage and unpacked only the necessities because there just wasn't enough space inside. As we twisted and turned our way through the eighteen-inch-wide pathway to get into our rental home each day, Mom would say things like, "This is only temporary. It won't be much longer. Soon we'll be in a better place and these boxes won't be here anymore."

A few weeks passed, then a few years, then a decade. The boxes and totes remained in the garage. Our time in that pump house certainly did not feel like "a little while."

Years later, when my mom was valiantly fighting her way through a cancer diagnosis, I read the verse quoted from First Peter above. After watching my mom endure numerous surgeries, months of chemotherapy, weeks of radiation and recovery, and more years of various strains of chemo, her suffering did not seem as though it was lasting "a little while."

Even though the pain and heartache dragged on and I couldn't see the end, I asked the Lord to help me see that in comparison to eternity, the sufferings in this life really do last just a little while. In the grand scheme of things, our lives on this earth are but a breath compared to the life we will enjoy with God in glory.

One of my favorite passages to meditate on during my mom's illness was 2 Corinthians 4:17-18 (NIV): "For our light and momentary troubles are achieving for us an eternal glory that far outweighs them all. So we fix our eyes not on what is seen, but on what is unseen, since what is seen is temporary, but what is unseen is eternal."

I also resonated with the following excerpt from Jen Pollock Michel:

Home helps us outlast our sufferings. We can admit our disappointments, grieve our losses, but recognize, with stubborn joy, that they are *temporary*. When seasons of unwanted singleness or infertility persist, when our marriages end, when a child dies, when the doctor delivers an unwanted diagnosis, we remember this earth is the lineup to the real event, and grief is one sure symptom of exile.[57]

When we focus on heaven, our anticipation can far outweigh the cares and scars of this world and cause the hurts to pale in comparison to the glory we will behold. When I struggle to allow the hope of eternity to "far outweigh" my earthly burdens, the Lord often reminds me of this hymn stanza:

Turn your eyes upon Jesus,
Look full in His wonderful face,
And the things of earth will grow strangely dim,
In the light of His glory and grace.[58]

I think back to my mom's initial promise when we moved into our rental cottage when I was young. No matter the situation, it wouldn't hurt to hold a similar perspective about life in general: "This is only temporary. It won't be much longer. Soon we'll be in a better place."

QUESTION FOR REFLECTION

Which difficult situations in your life do not feel as if they are lasting only "a little while"? How can the Scriptures from today's entry give you hope and encouragement?

36

DISPLACED

By faith Abraham, when called to go to a place he would later receive as his inheritance, obeyed and went, even though he did not know where he was going.

HEBREWS 11:8 NIV

In the fall of 2023, my friend Katie experienced significant flooding in her home, to the point that she had to move out of her house until the contractors could fix all the damage and renovate the affected rooms. This may not seem like a big deal, except that Katie and her husband have five children and a dog. Their insurance company covered the costs for the whole family (minus the dog) to move into a hotel.

At first, they anticipated that the renovations would take about three weeks. Well, three weeks came and went, and the work had not even begun. Days and nights passed as they tried to make the most of their displacement. There was no kitchen, just a mini fridge, so they had no way of cooking their own food. They ate more takeout than they ever wanted to. What felt like a vacation for a few weeks became tedious after that. One month passed. Then two. The hardest part was not knowing when they could finally return home. Had they known the specific date when the work would be completed, they could have adjusted their expectations. However, the unknowns kept them dependent on the sustaining strength of the Lord. They made friends with the cleaning staff, rode the elevators for entertainment, and carried hotel ice buckets down the hallway to fill at the ice machine. Though they tried to make the most of their circumstances and stay positive, over time tensions increased and patience decreased.

Soon they realized the repairs on their home would not be completed before Christmas. They would have to spend Christmas day at the hotel. They had a small taste of what Mary and Joseph might have felt when they were displaced on that first Christmas—away from home, in challenging circumstances, with not enough room in "the inn."

We read in the second chapter of Matthew that Joseph and Mary were unexpectedly displaced a second time shortly after Jesus was born: "An angel of the Lord appeared to Joseph in a dream and said, 'Rise, take the child and his mother, and flee to Egypt, and remain there until I tell you, for Herod is about to search for the child, to destroy him'" (Matt. 2:13). Like Katie and her family, Joseph and Mary had no idea how long they would have to stay away from their home. But they obeyed the command of the Lord: "And he rose and took the child and his mother by night and departed to Egypt and remained there until the death of Herod" (Matt. 2:14-15).

By the time the renovations on Katie's home were

finally completed in January of 2024, their family had spent 102 days sleeping, waking, eating, living, and breathing in that hotel—*102 days*. Needless to say, they were extremely happy to move home.

While I would never wish this kind of ordeal on anyone, it does make me think about how we might feel when we finally get to move home with the Lord. We have no idea how many more days we have left in this broken and decaying place, but after living in this cramped, temporary dwelling that is not our own, imagine the joy and delight we will feel when we finally get to our true home and experience the spacious freedom that comes without any confinements from sin, shame, guilt, or pain. We will no longer have to choke down monotonous hotel breakfasts day after day or dig through disorderly suitcases to find a clean pair of underwear. There will be no more bickering among siblings or squabbles between spouses. No more floods or damaged floors. We will be fully restored to our intended state. We will be beyond happy, beyond content, beyond satisfied. We will be home with the One we were made for, dwelling with Him forever.

QUESTION FOR REFLECTION

When you feel tired of feeling displaced in this world, what truths can you cling to in order to renew your hope in the home that awaits you?

37

HUNGERING FOR HEAVEN

Truly, truly, I say to you, whoever believes has eternal life. I am the bread of life. Your fathers ate the manna in the wilderness, and they died. This is the bread that comes down from heaven, so that one may eat of it and not die. I am the living bread that came down from heaven. If anyone eats of this bread, he will live forever.

JOHN 6:47-51

When I had teenage boys at home, I was constantly trying to find and prepare foods that would actually fill their stomachs for more than five minutes at a time. When my youngest was in high school, he would come home from school, eat a full meal at 4:00 p.m., go to the gym, then come home three hours later and ask, "What's for supper?" As I offered him another full plate of food, he would thank me but add, "That's not gonna fill me."

With certain recipes I prepared for my family, I knew in advance that the substance was not sufficient to tide us over until morning. As expected, within two hours of finishing the evening meal, family members would amble into the kitchen scrounging for something more to eat. Their bellies had not been satiated.

Author and speaker Jackie Hill Perry delivered a humorous and poignant illustration in one of her talks, using the Olive Garden restaurant chain as a link to Christ:

> You get to Olive Garden, and you sit down at your table. They bring you a basket of breadsticks—the most delicious breadsticks you'll ever have in your entire life. … Now, they bring the bread out and you eat one breadstick, then you lose your absolute mind. You eat two breadsticks, you eat three breadsticks. God forbid they brought out the salad with the cheese. Your stomach is just full of stuff. And then they bring you a menu. … You make your order. Then when the waitress comes out with your meal, something strange happens where you realize that you don't even want what you thought that you wanted, and the reason that you don't want it anymore is because you consumed so much bread that you don't have the capacity for anything else. And that's what happens when people get the Bread of Life. That's what happens when people get Jesus, is that they are so full of His love, so full of His power, so full of His truth, so full of His grace, that they don't have the capacity for foolishness no more. … When you eat bread, it holds weight in your body. So Jesus is saying, "I ain't just here to save you, I'm also here to satisfy you."[59]

Can I say this is true for myself? Do I live as though I am fully satisfied by Christ alone? Do I truly hunger for the Bread of Life, or am I trying to satisfy my appetite with temporary, worldly fare?

We are living in the foretaste of heaven. While many aspects of our experience on earth are beautiful, delightful, and satisfying, they're only the appetizer. "This life was never meant to 'fill us up'; it is only created to prepare us for the 'main course.'"[60]

Any cravings we may have for tangible satisfaction on earth will only achieve fleeting fulfillment. There will always be a hunger for more. But one day soon, we won't have to paw through the refrigerator at night looking for something extra to quell the rumbling in our stomachs. God Himself can and does and will fill the void and fully satisfy—like Olive Garden breadsticks.

QUESTION FOR REFLECTION

If you're honest with yourself, what are you really hungering for? What temporary pleasures have you been filling your stomach with while you wait for the true main course?

38

CITIZENS OF HEAVEN

But our citizenship is in heaven.
And we eagerly await a Savior
from there, the Lord Jesus Christ.

PHILIPPIANS 3:20 NIV

I am an American citizen who married a South African citizen. When our biological children were born in Cape Town, all I had to do was go to the US Embassy to notify them of the births. We were issued a Consular Report of Birth Abroad, and the kids were granted US citizenship immediately. The process was more complicated and took a lot longer for our adopted son, but after jumping through all the government-enforced hoops, he was eventually granted American citizenship as well.

Spouses of US citizens are not given the same privileges. The process for foreign spouses to obtain that coveted blue passport is much more rigorous and requires a longer waiting period. In fact, for various reasons, my husband, Kagiso, and I had been married for eighteen years and had lived in Michigan for ten years before he finally obtained US citizenship.

During that period when Kagiso did not yet have his navy blue passport, anytime we traveled together from

South Africa to the United States, after we disembarked the plane, our family was forced to separate—the kids and I filed toward the line with the sign that read "United States Citizens," and my husband had to break from his family to join the other queue.

Especially when we both lived in South Africa and Kagiso did not yet have a green card, this division was often cause for concern. What if I got into a car accident and had to be hospitalized in America while he was in South Africa and couldn't come to me immediately? At the height of the global pandemic, many borders were closed to anyone who didn't hold citizenship in that country. We were thankful that we weren't separated at that time, but many families were.

According to the Bible, there will be a point of separation on judgment day—the sheep and the goats:

> When the Son of Man comes in his glory, and all the angels with him, then he will sit on his glorious throne. Before him will be gathered all the nations, and he will separate people one from another as a shepherd separates the sheep from the goats. And he will place the sheep on his right, but the goats on the left. Then the King will say to those on his right, "Come, you who are blessed by my Father, inherit the kingdom prepared for you from the foundation of the world." … Then he will say to those on his left, "Depart from me, you cursed, into the eternal fire prepared for the devil and his angels." … And

> these will go away into eternal punishment, but the righteous into eternal life. (Matt. 25:31-34, 41, 46)

But for those who are in Christ, who have been covered by His blood, there will be no separate lines at the airport, no border control uniforms, no tired and agitated customs officials. My husband and I rejoiced and let out a mutual sigh of relief when he finally obtained his American citizenship after so many years. We would no longer have to go our separate ways at the airport. Even more so, we thank God for the immeasurable cost He paid by sacrificing His Son on the cross so we could gain access to Him—now and forever.

But what about other loved ones? Earthly citizenship is temporary. A day is coming when the passport you carry will mean nothing. What are you doing to ensure that your family, friends, and acquaintances have obtained the only passport that matters—the one given by Jesus Christ Himself through faith in Him, sealed with the promise of the Holy Spirit?

There's still time to share the good news with those who are lost, so that when the day of separation comes, you will walk together into the eternal Kingdom prepared for you, by His grace.

QUESTION FOR REFLECTION

Which citizenship do you value more—your earthly citizenship or your heavenly one?

39

STAMP OF APPROVAL

In him you also, when you heard the word of truth,
the gospel of your salvation, and believed in him,
were sealed with the promised Holy Spirit,
who is the guarantee of our inheritance until we
acquire possession of it, to the praise of his glory.

EPHESIANS 1:13-14

When I was living in South Africa, my husband and I were invited to an American Thanksgiving gathering with several fellow Americans. I was excited to mingle with recognizable accents and taste familiar holiday dishes, even if the recipes did have to be modified slightly due to our inability to access all the ingredients that are available in the States.

As we congregated around the table, someone brought up the topic of visa applications. Let me just tell you: whenever you get a group of missionaries or expats together, just say the word "visa" and you will be met with impassioned stories and conversations that last well into the night. This occasion was no exception. Voices clamored over each other to share their frustrating and sometimes downright outrageous stories related to their personal experiences trying to get in and out of foreign countries.

My husband and I held our own vat full of stories we had accumulated over the years. When we were applying for him to travel to the United States for our wedding ceremony, the application process dragged on much longer than anticipated. We had no choice but to continue with our wedding plans as if he were going to be granted the necessary paperwork in time, but at the back of our minds dwelled the nagging reality that there was no guarantee. My groom might not make it to his own wedding.

Other friends of ours had served as missionaries in a foreign country for more than a decade without any visa trouble. Then one day—during a regular renewal application they had received favorably countless times before—the government unexpectedly said no. They had to leave the country for a while and reapply, unsure of whether they would be granted reentry into the place that had become their home.

In a similar way, some of us may struggle with doubts as to whether the immigration officials in heaven will look favorably upon our paperwork and give us the stamp of approval to cross the border into paradise. Will we really be granted entry when we arrive at the gates of glory? What if our visa applications are denied? What if we get a crabby border control officer who didn't get enough sleep last night and woke up on the wrong side of the bed?

No, the Bible tells us that as soon as we believed in Christ by grace through faith, we were "sealed with the promised Holy Spirit" (Eph. 1:13). Our passports have already been stamped, and there is no expiration date and no need to reapply. The ink has dried and cannot be erased.

After my mom passed away, my sister and I learned that we were the beneficiaries of her life insurance policy and would each receive a modest sum as a result of her death. Technically that inheritance belonged to us before we even knew it existed. Then after we learned of its existence, we still weren't immediately aware of the amount we would receive. We had a basic understanding that an inheritance was ours, but we didn't know the extent of it. Even after we learned more about the scope, there was a period in which we knew it was ours, we understood what it would look like, but it had not yet reached our bank accounts. We had not yet acquired possession of it. Yet even before the balance in our accounts increased, the inheritance belonged to us. No one could claim it or take it away.

Similarly, the Lord Himself has given us a glorious inheritance in Christ. We cannot even fathom the extent of its impact or magnitude. And while we have not yet received it in full, the Bible tells us that the Holy Spirit serves as "the guarantee of our inheritance until we acquire possession of it" (Eph. 1:14). No one can take it away. No one can deny the stamp of entry into His eternal Kingdom. No border officials will keep us from crossing into what has already been prepared for us through the sacrifice of Jesus Christ.

QUESTION FOR REFLECTION

Describe a time when you doubted whether you would be granted entrance into the Lord's presence in glory.

40

GREAT EXPECTATIONS

Come and see what God has done.

PSALM 66:5

When our family moved from South Africa to Michigan in January 2013, we caught the tail end of winter. We had just enough snow in February to put the brand-new shovels to good use and crack a couple of sleds on the hill across the road. By October of 2013, however, after a glorious summer and far too many leaves to rake, the first snow glistened in the streetlights of the still-dark morning. When my kids woke up and saw the dusting of white powder on the ground, they were so excited they nearly ran outside in their pajamas without any shoes on their feet. More snow followed. And more. Snowstorm after snowstorm, inch after inch, week after week, and month after month until our region broke the snowfall records held for over thirty years.

My eldest son's birthday is at the end of March, and in January he asked me, "Hey Mom, will it still be snowing on my birthday?" Having grown up in Michigan, I quickly and confidently answered, "No. It will all be gone by then."

Well, I was wrong.

At the end of March that year, the fluffy white stuff that had once been so enchanting was in its sixth month and *still* falling, and it was losing its appeal by the hour. In the first week of April we finally had some rain, and the mountains of previously plowed snow diminished much more quickly than expected. Then one day I parked my minivan on a street downtown and suddenly my six-year-old exclaimed, *"LOOK!"* The magnitude of his outburst was so great, I expected to see something mind-blowing and unimaginable. Instead, I turned my head in the direction his finger was pointing and spotted tips of green emerging from the dirt. Just when we thought we'd never see it again, we began to witness shoots of life springing up from the earth. My son was ecstatic. For weeks afterward, every time anything green caught his eye, he would shout with just as much vigor as he did with that first sighting. He was just *that* excited to see the promise of new life.

My daughter's enthusiasm for spring rivaled her brother's, though her excitement was seated in a slightly different motivation—she wanted to wear her dresses. At the first hint that the mercury in the outdoor thermometer might crane its neck to eke above the fifty-degree mark, she would fall to her knees and beg and plead until I caved and let her wear a short-sleeved dress without tights and without a long-sleeved shirt underneath or a cardigan on top. Then she floated outside like a brand-new butterfly freshly freed from its cocoon. She flitted her wings and soared around the backyard and into the driveway, the brisk air dancing into her stale winter lungs.

Then there was my eldest, twelve at the time, who took every opportunity to ask, "Please can we go outside to Rollerblade in the church parking lot?" and "Can we play soccer in the backyard?" and "Could we go for a walk or a bike ride?"

As I watched my kids and their tangible anticipation for warmth and growth and fresh air after months of being cooped up inside, a deeper longing for heaven grew within me. I started to see snippets of what it's like to really, *really* look forward to something—something longer-lasting than Christmas morning. Something like the spreading of wings after being wrapped up in a cocoon for days on end.

I began to imagine arriving in heaven after being confined to earth, seeing the wonder of new life for the first time, and exclaiming like my son, *"LOOK!"* But unlike the promise of shoots springing up from the earth, the delights of heaven will never fade. The flowers will never wilt after they bloom. The glories of paradise will just keep blooming forever and ever and ever, and our enjoyment will never diminish.

QUESTION FOR REFLECTION

In what ways does your excitement for earthly joys remind you of what you can look forward to in heaven?

41

SHELTER IN THE STORM

When the storm has swept by, the wicked are gone,
but the righteous stand firm forever.

PROVERBS 10:25 NIV

My family and I were on our way from Cape Town to Johannesburg, a sixteen-hour drive. As we crossed the border into a new province up-country, my husband rolled down the window and took in a deep breath.

"Ah, can you smell it?" he exhaled with deep satisfaction. "The air is different here. And it's going to rain—I can tell."

Sure enough, dark clouds soon appeared, moving in our direction. We pulled into a rest stop to satiate our hunger, and after looking at the fast-food menu, I lifted my head and caught a glimpse through the wall of windows into the parking lot. The weather was changing—and fast. Flags whipped uncontrollably, umbrellas on the outdoor tables flailed around, and people ran inside, holding onto hats, hair, and jackets.

I took one look at my husband and asked for the car keys. The wind was so strong I was barely able to move in a straight line as I ran to our vehicle. Already I could feel drops of rain landing on me. I grabbed a jacket for each of us, locked the car, and ran back to the restaurant, just in the nick of time.

Others who had been eating inside saw the weather and started to panic. They quickly paid their bills and rushed out the door, making a beeline for their vehicles.

"Should we try to beat it?" I asked my husband with a hint of apprehension in my voice.

"Nah, just relax. It's going to pass soon. I know this part of the country; that's what always happens. Besides, the kids are happy, let's let them play a little longer."

I agreed, but it certainly did not look like this storm was going anywhere anytime soon, and I was not looking forward to riding shotgun while he navigated through torrents of rain on a two-lane highway.

We stayed at the table for another half hour while other customers sprinted in and out, drenched with rain through and through.

The next thing I knew, I looked out the window and the sky was clearing! I couldn't believe it. Not even an hour had passed, and in my experience, a storm as nasty as that was never brief. But my husband was a seasoned veteran of those parts. He was familiar with the weather patterns, and if he were a gambling man, he could've put money on the duration of the storm. Unlike the rest of us, who were in a state of mild frenzy, he remained calm and sat peacefully in the shelter of the walls and roof that surrounded him.

Storms in life tend to elicit varied responses, don't they? Some of us immediately panic and flail around, trying to run away from the storm. Others, perhaps more seasoned and familiar with the nature of hardship, are more likely to rest in a secure shelter with a firm foundation and wait for the storm to pass.

Those who trust in the Lord can cling to the beautiful promise of a safe and secure refuge in Christ: "You have been a refuge for the poor, a refuge for the needy in their distress, a shelter from the storm and a shade from the heat" (Isa. 25:4 NIV).

On that day on the side of the road in South Africa, I was prone to worry and anxiety, but my husband's temperament mirrored that of the psalmist David: "Be merciful to me, O God, be merciful to me, for in you my soul takes refuge; in the shadow of your wings I will take refuge, till the storms of destruction pass by" (Ps. 57:1).

We have a choice: we can attempt to outrun the disaster in our own strength, or we can hide in the shadow of His wings and trust that He will guard and shield us until the disaster has passed.

The reality is, as long as we're here on this earth, storms and disasters are going to keep coming. We may experience a temporary reprieve, but the next storm will always be in the not-too-distant forecast.

Yet we can all look forward to the day when the final storm passes by and there will be no more threat of darkness. We will be welcomed into the light without fear of damage done by torrential floods, cracks of lightning, or gale-force winds. We will be safe forever in the presence of the Maker of all, and He will be our greatest delight.

QUESTION FOR REFLECTION

When you experience storms in life, do you tend to take shelter in the Lord or attempt to outrun the storm in your own strength?

42

UNMET EXPECTATIONS

Blessed are those who hunger and thirst for righteousness, for they shall be satisfied.
MATTHEW 5:6

Most of us can think of a time when the excited build-up to a much-anticipated event swelled so great that it swallowed up the event itself, like a surfer being sucked in by a crashing wave. We can so elevate our expectations that we set ourselves up for disappointment when the big day finally arrives, and the reality ends up being a major letdown.

A similar situation happened to the character Marly in Virginia Sorensen's book *Miracles on Maple Hill*. Her whole childhood up to that day had been filled with her mama's memories of great-grandma's house at Maple Hill—delightful stories that sounded almost too good to be true. Marly bubbled over with excitement as her family finally traveled the road leading up to this much-talked-about destination. Her expectations soared, and Marly fully anticipated miracles to happen in that magical place. Once they got there, however, her hopes were put to the test:

> But it looked little and old to be all that. She was afraid, now that she was actually here, that it wasn't. She wished that they were still on the way. Sometimes even Christmas wasn't as much fun as getting ready for it. Maybe thinking about Maple Hill would turn out to be better than Maple Hill itself.[61]

I felt a similar disappointment when my husband and I celebrated our twentieth wedding anniversary. I had planned a two-night getaway for us to a hotel suite I'd wanted to visit for more than four years. The timing had never worked out until that year, and I was so excited to take him to the place that had captured my interest. However, once we arrived, I learned that the pictures in the advertisements must have been rather outdated. Instead of what I expected to find based on the photos I saw online, the entire complex was in various stages of disrepair and looked worn out and run down.

These kinds of disappointments happen often in this life, where we live in the shadow of things to come. But they will never happen in heaven. No matter how high our expectations of paradise, we will never be disappointed. Even our greatest imaginings will pale in comparison to the glory to be revealed in the life to come.

I appreciate the following excerpt from Joni Eareckson Tada's book *Heaven: Your Real Home*:

> For me, true contentment on earth means asking less of this life because more is coming in the next. Godly

> contentment is great gain. Heavenly gain. Because God has created the appetites in your heart, it stands to reason that He must be the consummation of that hunger. Yes, heaven will galvanize your heart if you focus your faith not on a place of glittery mansions, but on a Person, Jesus, who makes heaven a home.[62]

May the Lord help us to yearn and hunger with a heavenward hope, with cravings only He can fully satisfy.

QUESTION FOR REFLECTION

Describe a time when your expectations were let down, then say or write a prayer of thanksgiving to God, acknowledging that this type of disappointment will never happen when you arrive in glory.

43

WALKING IN HIS LIGHT

And the city has no need of sun or moon to shine on it, for the glory of God gives it light, and its lamp is the Lamb.

REVELATION 21:23

When my mom was sick with cancer in Michigan while I lived in Cape Town, I traveled with my three kids to visit her. My sister graciously opened her home to us. That first night after traveling almost thirty-six hours from door to door, I settled my kids—ages nine, six, and four at the time—into their respective guest bedrooms before gratefully sinking into the air mattress my sister had prepared for me in a separate room.

As soon as my head hit the pillow, I fell into a deep sleep. After an unknown number of hours, I woke in the pitch darkness to the faint, muffled sound of my youngest son's voice. Was I dreaming? I listened and heard my four-year-old calling for me again. The room I was in was so dark, I couldn't even see my hand in front of my face. In my jet-lagged, sleep-deprived stupor, I clumsily rolled off the air mattress onto the carpeted floor and crawled in the general direction of the door. I could hear my son calling from the next room, but I couldn't find the door to get out of the room I was in. From my hands and knees, I groped along the wall searching for a door frame. "I'm coming!" I called out to him. "I'm coming! I just can't find the door!"

I felt trapped and helpless. My son was in need, and I couldn't get to him. I finally found the wooden door but couldn't find the handle. I reached and reached in the darkness, frantically flailing my arms until finally—finally!—I found the handle and managed to open the door.

As it turned out, somehow my four-year-old had fallen off the bottom bunk, managed to roll underneath the bed, and couldn't figure out how to get out. If only I had been able to see, I could've reached him much more quickly.

Through that somewhat harrowing experience, I realized the vital role of light in our lives. When we're in darkness, we flail around on our hands and knees, groping at walls to try to find a doorknob that we can't see. We're trapped when we're in darkness. We can't move at all, let alone move forward in a healthy direction.

In John 8:12 (NIV), we read, "When Jesus spoke again to the people, he said, 'I am the light of the world. Whoever follows me will never walk in darkness, but will have the light of life.'" In Christ, we don't have to crawl around in darkness. He illuminates our path and shines His light on the way we should go.

Based on the passage above from Revelation 21, we will soon experience the full extent of the light of Christ in glory. He will illuminate the whole Celestial City.

Imagine a place with no need for the sun!

I'm embarrassed to admit that I didn't even think to pray and ask God for help when I was trapped in literal darkness in my sister's house. Though I failed to seek His light in that situation, it was not too late to turn to Him in the future. If you feel as though you're groping around in a season of spiritual darkness, ask the Lord to illuminate your path, to shed light on your circumstances, and to help you find the doorknob to reach Him. May He continue to increase our desire for that day when we'll live forever in the light of His truth and grace.

QUESTION FOR REFLECTION

Describe an experience when you felt you were in darkness (literally or figuratively) and couldn't find your way out. Did you turn to the Lord for help at that time, asking Him to shed light on your circumstances?

44

HOMESICK FOR HEAVEN

For in this tent we groan, longing to put on our heavenly dwelling.

2 CORINTHIANS 5:2

It's what happens when you grow up on the Atlantic seaboard and get relocated to landlocked Nebraska cornfields. On that long-awaited return to the coast, when that familiar saltiness of the air reaches your nostrils before seagulls are sighted—you know that you're *home*.

It's what happens when you've been away on a business trip, and your aircraft descends through the blanket of clouds so you can see the familiar, sweeping landscape below—and you know that you're *home*.

It's what happens when you've been cooped up in a college dorm for an entire semester, and it's finally Christmas break. You open the front door to your childhood house, and the smell of freshly baked chocolate chip cookies wafts through the cozy atmosphere—and you know that you're *home*.

I have to wonder if we won't have that same feeling—only magnified infinitely—when we get to heaven.

As Alcorn observes:

> We are homesick for Eden. We're nostalgic for what's implanted in our hearts. It's built into us, perhaps even at a genetic level. We long for what the first man and woman enjoyed—a perfect and beautiful Earth with free and untainted relationships with God, each other, animals, and our environment. Every attempt at human progress has been an attempt to overcome what was lost in the Fall.[63]

I once saw the most remarkable video of an infant, just minutes after birth. She had been placed skin-to-skin on her mother's abdomen, shock of black hair still matted with remnants of amniotic fluid. With eyes clenched shut, the newborn managed to inch her way upward, squirming like a worm. Slowly, gradually, this baby wriggled and grunted along her mother's body until she found the source of the milk—and she began to drink.

Deep down, in the hollows of our own hearts, we know there is milk to be found. We can smell it. We long for it.

Consider this excerpt from E. M. Bounds:

> At home in heaven! What welcome! What satisfaction! What rest to tired feet, and tired hearts! What a sense of security and confidence! The home feelings in full opulence of richest wealth! Nowhere on earth's green, glad soil will the home feeling be so profound, so satisfying, so restful, and so happifying as in heaven. It is not only to be realized as home

> when we get there, but all along the way the home feeling is to draw and bind us to that heavenly world. The homesickness for heaven is to alienate us from earth, make us sick at heart and beget pinings for home.[64]

I don't know what it will be like when we get to heaven, but I have a feeling that upon arrival, we'll just know that we're finally *home*. We'll know that we've finally inched our way to the source of the rich milk that has nourished us for all these years.

QUESTION FOR REFLECTION

How would you articulate
the homesickness you feel for heaven?

45

MAKING MUD PIES

In your presence there is fullness of joy;
at your right hand are pleasures forevermore.
PSALM 16:11

After my mom died, I caught myself entertaining irrational thoughts. When it was a beautiful day outside, I would think, *Oh, what a pity that Mom is missing such a glorious day. She would have loved this blue sky and sunshine.* Then I would realize my fallacy. The weather is infinitely and permanently better in heaven. This world is but a shadow. I would drive past one of Mom's favorite restaurants and think, *How disappointing that she'll never be able to eat chicken pad thai from Thai Palace or Mongolian beef from Mr. You's Chinese takeout.* Then the Lord would correct my thinking, and I would concede that the food must be much better in glory. The Chinese buffet on earth has nothing on heaven's buffet.

I love the imagery that C. S. Lewis paints of our nearsightedness in this life:

> It would seem that Our Lord finds our desires not too strong, but too weak. We are half-hearted creatures, fooling about with drink and sex and ambition

> when infinite joy is offered us, like an ignorant child who wants to go on making mud pies in a slum because he cannot imagine what is meant by the offer of a holiday at the sea. We are far too easily pleased.[65]

Isn't it true? We not only settle for the temporary pleasures of this world, but we elevate those pleasures to positions they have neither earned nor deserve. Whenever I'm tempted to think it's a pity that my mom is missing out on earthly enjoyments such as Chinese takeout or a sunset picnic at the beach, I'm making mud pies. In those moments, my view of heaven is severely and grossly distorted.

The following excerpts from separate prayers in the collection *The Valley of Vision* can help us calibrate our malfunctioning compasses:

> O Lord,
> I live here as a fish in a vessel of water,
> only enough to keep me alive,
> but in heaven I shall swim in the ocean.
> Here I have a little air in me to keep me breathing,
> but there I shall have sweet and fresh gales;
> Here I have a beam of sun to lighten my darkness,
> a warm ray to keep me from freezing;
> yonder I shall live in light and warmth for ever.[66]

> May I arrive …
> Where the more perfect the sight
> the more beautiful the object,

The more perfect the appetite
  the sweeter the food,
The more musical the ear
  the more pleasant the melody,
The more complete the soul
  the more happy its joys,
Where is full knowledge of thee.[67]

My finite brain cannot comprehend a place that is perfect in every way. Even the most astounding, unimaginable expectations we may have about heaven will fall short of the reality we experience when we arrive.

QUESTION FOR REFLECTION

In what ways have you caught yourself having limiting views of heaven?

46

WATCHING WITH HOPE

But as for me, I watch in hope for the LORD*,*
I wait for God my Savior; my God will hear me.

MICAH 7:7 NIV

Have you ever watched a dog eagerly anticipating the arrival of its owner? My friend Carol told me about a time when she was staying at our mutual friend Gaby's home overnight. Carol was sleeping on the couch in the living area, and suddenly Gaby's German shepherd jumped up and ran excitedly to the sliding door at the front of the house.

"What do you see?" Carol asked the dog. Carol didn't see anything unusual through the glass pane. Then a few seconds later, she saw Gaby's lime green Volkswagen Beetle making its way up the hill toward the driveway. The dog had heard its owner's car before it was even visible and went running for the front door, whimpering and panting with unbridled excitement, tail beating hard against the carpet.

Am I listening with the same intent for my Savior's coming? Will my excitement match Gaby's German shepherd when I hear the sound of His arrival drawing near?

As soon as my South African mother-in-law and

brother-in-law received their visas to visit us in America for the first time ever—five months before they intended to travel—I started counting the days until their arrival. When the day finally came for their transatlantic plane to land, I drove three hours from our home in Michigan to O'Hare International Airport in Chicago to pick them up. The notification "LANDED" appeared on the screen in the arrivals terminal, and I was so excited I could hardly contain myself. I asked a security officer where I should stand to see them as soon as possible, and she directed me to the bottom of a one-way escalator. I planted myself at the bottom of this slow-moving apparatus, with no way of getting any closer or seeing them any faster. I watched as person after person, tired body after tired body, stepped onto the top of the escalator and began their slow descent to the platform where I stood waiting rather impatiently. Minutes ticked by, and with each passing second, my anticipation grew. They were almost here!

When I finally saw their familiar faces on the escalator, I actually jumped with excitement. I danced from side to side and waved my arms, not caring who saw me or what they thought of my dramatic antics. The wait was finally over!

If I can experience that level of excitement when loved ones arrive after a long separation, how much more should I be jumping up and down in anticipation of the future coming of my Lord? The following illustration gives a hint of what that anticipation is like.

> In one of his books, A. M. Hunter relates the story of a dying man who asked his Christian doctor to tell him something about the place to which he was going. As the doctor fumbled for a reply, he heard a scratching at the door, and he had his answer. "Do you hear that?" he asked his patient. "It's my dog. I left him downstairs, but he has grown impatient, and has come up and hears my voice. He has no notion what is inside this door, but he knows that I am here. Isn't it the same with you? You don't know what lies beyond the door, but you know that your Master is there."[68]

It may seem challenging to muster up a tangible excitement for the next life because we don't know what to expect. But we do know who we will find there, and the anticipation of being in His presence alone should cause a great sense of eagerness and expectation to swell within us. Our Master is there, and the wait will soon be over.

QUESTION FOR REFLECTION

On a scale of one to ten, how would you rate your level of excitement and anticipation for the Lord's coming? What can you do to increase that number?

47

A LIVING HOPE

Blessed be the God and Father of our Lord Jesus Christ! According to his great mercy, he has caused us to be born again to a living hope through the resurrection of Jesus Christ from the dead.

1 PETER 1:3

When my kids were younger, we used to make paper chains when we wanted to count down to a special occasion such as Christmas or a long-awaited vacation. Each morning we would tear off one of the links in the chain as a visible sign that the wait was now a bit shorter than it had been the day before. The much-anticipated event had grown just a little bit nearer, and our excitement increased with each torn piece of paper.

When I'm waiting for something important and valuable to arrive in the mail, I stalk the mailman every morning between 10:00 a.m. and 11:00 a.m., eager to see his white truck turn into the neighborhood. I barely give him time to close my mailbox before I'm in the driveway, speed-walking to the street to see whether my package arrived.

On other occasions, however, I have ordered items online that were rather inconsequential, and I easily forgot that I had even placed an order. Days passed, and I never gave my purchase a second thought until I was surprised to see a cardboard box at my doorstep.

At times, our view of heaven and eternity with God can lean more toward the inconsequential, forgotten purchase rather than the much-anticipated piece of mail. We go about our days, busy and occupied with many distractions, failing to care enough to check the mailbox or the front door.

In one sermon I heard, the preacher pointed out, "We often live like we forgot that we're expecting something."[69] Instead, our hope should be a *living* hope, as if we're eagerly watching for the mailman, wondering if today will be the day we receive our inheritance. In this broken world filled with broken people who are prone to forgetfulness, "hope has to be maintained; hope has to be fought for."[70] As we fight for hope, perhaps we can remind ourselves to daily "check the mail," anticipating that today could be the day we receive the greatest package of all—the gift of eternity with God.

In 1488, a Portuguese navigator named Bartolomeu Dias traveled by ship around the southern tip of the Cape Peninsula in South Africa. Due to the tumultuous nature of the weather and seas, he named the place "Cape of Storms." Later, King John II of Portugal wanted to highlight the appeal of this recently discovered route to access India by sea. He looked ahead, saw the promise of treasures in India, and renamed the place "Cape of Good Hope." When we focus only on our present circumstances, we will likely think of our own lives as a "Cape of Storms," of sorts. But when we intentionally look beyond this moment to what lies ahead in Christ and who we will find there, we realize this life is actually a "Cape of Good Hope."[71]

As we persevere through this life full of storms, we can keep counting down the days in anticipation like the paper chains counting down to Christmas, because every day we're one step closer to eternity. And *that* should make us excited.

QUESTION FOR REFLECTION

In what ways can you actively practice the "paper chain" mentality in order to maintain your living hope for the life to come?

48

GOD'S WAITING ROOM

I wait for the LORD, *my soul waits, and in his word I hope; my soul waits for the Lord more than watchmen for the morning, more than watchmen for the morning.*

PSALM 130:5-6

In 2022, I ended up going to the emergency department at a local hospital because of ongoing pain and discomfort that could not be resolved. I hadn't been to that particular hospital as a patient before, and as soon as I arrived at the registration desk and saw the overflowing waiting room, I knew I should have chosen a different facility nearby. I had arrived around 6:00 p.m. on a weekday, thinking it wouldn't be very busy. I was wrong. The nurse said the wait would be at least a few hours, maybe more, so I told my husband to go home and come back for me when I was finished.

While I waited, more and more people came through the doors. The nurses continued to rearrange the bodies in the room, pushing wheelchairs this way and that to accommodate more individuals. Each time a nurse came through the entryway to call another patient, my head perked up in hopes that my name would be called next. I eagerly awaited my turn. Time after time, I was disappointed. Two hours. Three hours. Hopes dashed. Pain increasing. Patience waning. Ice pack melting. Four hours. Then five. If I didn't have a clock on my cell phone, I would've had no idea in the windowless room whether it was morning or night.

As I sat in the borrowed hospital wheelchair, I imagined how long the nights must have felt for the shepherds and watchmen back in biblical times. They didn't have a wristwatch or an iPhone they could whip out of their pocket to see what time it was. Instead, they had to wait. *Is it morning yet? Is that a hint of light at the horizon? Is daylight almost here?* As an impatient patient in the ER, I could only imagine their anticipation and relief when they finally saw the sun.

My mom spent the final three months of her earthly life in a residential hospice care facility. We were blessed to have such a gorgeous and wonderful resource at our disposal, with caring nurses who met her needs with grace and love and did all they could to make my mom as comfortable as possible. They allowed her to bring things from her house that would make her room feel more cozy and familiar. But as much as they tried to make it seem like "home," it was what it was—a holding cell.

A waiting room for eternity.

A building permeated with the smell of death.

Once when I was really struggling as I watched my mom's suffering and decline, a family friend who was also a doctor and anatomy professor helped me to realign my perspective. He reminded me, "We're all terminally ill.

From birth, we're all receiving palliative care."

Hebrews 9:27 tells us that all men are appointed to die once, and then to face judgment. Whether we realize it or not, we're all sitting in the waiting room for eternity. Some of us are further along in the queue than others, but one day the door will open, and the nurse will call out, "Ms. So-and-So, He'll see you now."

When the time comes, we would be wise to make sure that we're waiting for the right doctor—not someone who is unable to help and sends us home in the same condition as before (or worse). Only one Great Physician can heal completely and bring the good news of everlasting life.

QUESTION FOR REFLECTION

As you sit in the waiting room of eternity,
what steps do you need to take to be
ready for the Lord to call your name?

OUR DWELLING PLACE

And I saw no temple in the city, for its temple is the Lord God the Almighty and the Lamb.

REVELATION 21:22

Throughout the Bible, we see various ways in which the Lord dwells with His people. In the Old Testament, He walks with Adam and Eve in the Garden of Eden (Gen. 3:8). His people build altars when He reveals His presence to them. He instructs them to build a tent or tabernacle for Him (Exod. 25:8). When they are traveling, He dwells among them in the form of fire and a cloud (Exod. 13:21), and also in a special way surrounding the Ark of the Covenant (Exod. 25:22). Eventually, God gives very specific instructions about the Temple that is to be built for His dwelling place (1 Chron. 28).

In the New Testament, we read about the Holy Spirit dwelling in God's people (John 14:16-17; Rom. 8:11; 1 Cor. 3:16-17; 2 Tim. 1:14), and how the Church, the body of Christ, is being built up to become a dwelling place for God (Eph. 2:19-22). But ultimately, each of these variations are pointing toward a greater, future reality: the eternal presence of the Lord in glory.

As Nancy Guthrie explains,

> The real sanctuary of God … is not where the masonry is; it's where God is. I think Moses understood this many years before this when he composed Psalm 90, when he wrote, "Lord, you have been our dwelling place in all generations." … The longing we have to be at home isn't necessarily so much the longing for a place, but the longing for a person.

In her book *The Promise Is His Presence: Why God Is Always Enough*, author Glenna Marshall paints this beautiful picture:

> Remember the temple curtain that ripped when Jesus died? In heaven the curtain is as noticeably absent as the temple structure is, because *God* is the sanctuary. He is the dwelling place—our dwelling place. He is the gift of heaven. His presence is the treasure. He is the song we will sing for eternity, because He will be our full satisfaction for the infinite days going forward. Our neediness will be obliterated in the face of His imminent, vibrant, eternity-filling *presence*. All the ways He pushed through our sinfulness and resistance were tastes—glimpses—shadows of the fullness of His presence we will enjoy in heaven. He is our inheritance. We will be free from any need or longing or yearning, because we will be free and face-to-face with the God we have yearned for since the day Adam fell.[72]

Many of us spend a significant amount of time and energy in this life trying to feel settled, trying to find a place where we feel we belong. Could it be that we've been looking in all the wrong places, with a distorted picture in our minds of what it means to feel at home?

Yes, there will be a glorious, indescribable, real place that God has prepared for us—but the object of our affection should not and will not be the place. The object of our affection, adoration, worship, awe, and praise will be God Himself—and *He* will be our dwelling place.

QUESTION FOR REFLECTION

In what ways have you been trying to create a place for yourself here on earth, or perhaps had a distorted view of what heaven will be like when you arrive?

50

NO MORE

He will wipe every tear from their eyes. There will be no more death or mourning or crying or pain, for the old order of things has passed away.

REVELATION 21:4 NIV

As I was writing this book, a friend of ours—a *young*, vibrant friend of ours—was diagnosed with an aggressive form of cancer. Stage four. While she was seven months pregnant with her third daughter. She fought valiantly for a full year before the cancer took her at age thirty-two.

On the day his precious wife died, my friend's husband announced her death on Facebook with a single sentence, followed by two passages of Scripture:

"She is home with Jesus."

She is *home* with Jesus.

She is home *with Jesus*.

The hope of home. The hope of His presence.

Throughout their yearlong, heart-wrenching battle with a vicious disease, this dear couple never lost their hope in the Lord. Their testimonies did not waver. His sustaining grace held them fast.

And now, despite a tremendous and immeasurable sense of loss for those left behind, this amazing woman who radiated the light of Christ is home with Jesus.

Hebrews 6:19 (NIV) says, "We have this hope as an anchor for the soul, firm and secure." While commenting on the passage from Revelation quoted at the beginning of this entry, Timothy Keller described the vital importance of this anchor in his book, *Walking with God through Pain and Suffering*:

> There is nothing more practical for sufferers than to have hope. The erosion or loss of hope is what makes suffering unbearable. And here at the end of the Bible is the ultimate hope—a material world in which all suffering is gone—"every tear wiped from our eyes." This is a life-transforming, living hope.
>
> Who was John writing to in the book of Revelation? … He was writing to people who were experiencing death and mourning and crying and pain. This book was written near the end of the first century when we know the Roman emperor Domitian was conducting large-scale persecutions of Christians. Some had their homes taken away and plundered, while some were sent into the arena to be torn to pieces by wild beasts as the crowds watched. Others were impaled on stakes and, while still alive, covered with pitch and lit afire. That is what the readers of this book were facing.
>
> And what did John give them so they could face it all? John gave them the ultimate hope—a new heavens and a new earth that was coming. That is

> what he gave them to face it, and it is a simple fact of history that it worked. We know that the early Christians took their suffering with great poise and peace and they sang hymns as the beasts were tearing them apart and they forgave the people who were killing them. And so the more they were killed, the more the Christian movement grew. Why? Because when people watched Christians dying like that, they said, "These people have got something." Well, do you know what they had? They had this. It is a living hope.[73]

On the thirteenth anniversary of my mom's death to cancer, I shared the following on social media:

> Even after thirteen years, there are still things I wish I could tell her, show her, ask her, do with her.
>
> But then I think about some of the things that have happened in the past thirteen years in the world and in our extended family that would have likely crushed her and broken her heart, and I'm reminded of this quote from Elizabeth Prentiss's book, *Stepping Heavenward*:
>
> "My precious, precious mother has been a saint in Heaven more than two years, and has forgotten all the *battles* she fought on earth, and all her *sorrows* and all her *sufferings*—in the presence of her Redeemer. … My steadfast aim now is to *follow in my mother's footsteps*; to imitate her cheerfulness, her

benevolence, her bright, inspiring ways—and never to rest till in place of my selfish nature, I become as full of *Christ's love* as she became. I am glad she is at last relieved from the knowledge of all my cares, and though I often yearn to throw myself into her arms and pour out my cares and trials into her sympathizing ears—I would not have her back for all the world. She has got away from all the turmoil and suffering of life; let her stay!"[74]

Those we have loved and lost in the Lord are now free of all suffering, and those of us left behind who hope in Him are buoyed by the promise that one day soon "there will be no more death or mourning or crying or pain" (Rev. 21:4 NIV). Until then, we cling to the living, unshakable hope that God will continue to fulfill His promises.

QUESTION FOR REFLECTION

In what ways has God used your living hope in Him to sustain you in the midst of hardship?

51

CROSSING THE FINISH LINE

And I am sure of this, that he who began a good work in you will bring it to completion at the day of Jesus Christ.

PHILIPPIANS 1:6

When my kids were much younger, my almost-ten-year-old daughter decided it would be fun to participate in a local Color Run—a 5K race that involved bursts of colored powder being sprayed on runners at random intervals throughout the race. Sounds like fun, right? Well, somehow she persuaded my sister to do the race with her, and before I knew what was happening, my eight-year-old son Caleb and I were registered as well.

Of the four of us, my sister was the only one who had ever participated in an organized race—or run more than one mile at a time. Mostly against their will, I dragged my kids on a couple of "training runs" to try to build up our endurance in a weak attempt to make the big day more bearable.

Two days before the race, we were relaxing at a friend's pool with a few other families. All of a sudden, I heard a loud noise followed by a shrill scream of pain. I jumped up and found Caleb lying on the ground, grabbing his foot, his hand covered in blood. He had been running on the pool deck and somehow managed to clip his toe on the edge of the railing. The force of the momentum caused the nail on his smallest toe to completely rip off.

My stomach turned just looking at it. He tried to be brave and strong, but clearly he was in a heap of pain. As we packed up our belongings and headed to the car, I realized it was highly unlikely that Caleb would be able to participate in the Color Run. We got home, cleaned up his wound, and bandaged it up the best we could, given the awkward location. The poor kid spent the rest of the afternoon on the couch watching TV with his foot propped up on a pillow.

Less than forty-eight hours later, Caleb was still limping along—but he was determined to run the race. Against my better judgment, we loaded into the minivan and drove the forty-five minutes from home at some unpleasantly early hour to get to the starting line in time. My daughter—the adrenaline junkie who got us into this mess in the first place—bubbled with excitement and enthusiasm.

I waited until we arrived at the crowded venue to attempt to put a real shoe onto Caleb's injured foot. Until that moment, he had been wearing flip-flops with bare feet, so as not to aggravate his wounded toe. My efforts to slip his foot into an athletic shoe as gently and gingerly as possible didn't help; the sock alone was enough for the pain to escalate.

"Are you sure you want to do this?" I asked him from

the parked car. "Mm-hmm," he replied through gritted teeth.

The starting gun fired, and we joined the masses of runners passing through the gate to begin the race. Poor Caleb limped and hobbled and groaned in discomfort alongside me. It quickly became clear that he was not going to be able to run or even jog at a comfortable speed, so I told my sister to go ahead with my daughter and I would follow behind with Caleb.

Let me just say, those were three long miles. What was supposed to be a fun, color-filled experience became an agonizing, drawn-out forty-five minutes of torment for my injured son. I tried to distract him from his pain by pointing out cool things along the route and reminding him of funny stories from the past, but nothing worked. He was miserable.

After what felt like hours, the finish line was finally in sight. As soon as he hobbled over the line, a huge smile spread across his face. He had done it.

Once it was over, the memories of the agony soon diminished, replaced by a victory T-shirt commemorating the Color Run and a medal proudly worn around his neck.

In November 2021, marathon runner Jamel Melville was 650 feet from the finish line of the TCS New York City Marathon when his legs gave out and he collapsed on the route. Before the medical personnel could reach him, two strangers ran past, stopped their own race, and turned around to lift him up and carry him to the end of the route so he could finish the race.[75]

Perhaps you feel as if your toenail has been ripped off or your legs are about to give out. If that's the case, cling to this promise: Even if we are hobbling and limping and crying all the way to the end, the Lord has promised to carry us across the finish line.

QUESTION FOR REFLECTION

In what ways are you depending on the Lord to carry you across the finish line?

A RICH WELCOME

Therefore, my brothers and sisters, make every effort to confirm your calling and election. For if you do these things, you will never stumble, and you will receive a rich welcome into the eternal kingdom of our Lord and Savior Jesus Christ.

2 PETER 1:10-11 NIV

In his book *Eternity: Reclaiming a Passion for What Endures*, Joseph Stowell shares the moving story of "an elderly missionary couple who arrived at their home port after years of faithful service."

> At the dock, an ambassador and his wife who had returned on the ship with them were surrounded by a crowd. Roses were bestowed on his wife as photographers' flashes exploded, and an attentive, admiring press and public hung on every word as he spoke of the joy of serving his government and coming home. As the missionary couple walked unnoticed through the crowd, the wife, with hot tears streaking her face, wondered out loud to her husband, "Why is it that we have given our whole lives to Christ and yet there is no one here to honor us and welcome us home?"

> Her understanding husband, reaching beyond that lonely moment, said to her, "Honey, we're not home yet."[76]

We're not home yet.

Five years after my family and I moved from South Africa to the States, we decided to make the transatlantic trek to Cape Town for a visit. When the plane approached our destination, I wondered what it would be like to return after such a long time. Would we feel like strangers?

The aircraft landed, and we waited our turn to shuffle off the plane in a single-file line. We followed the masses of people down the sterile corridor until we turned a corner and saw it—a huge group of our friends and family stood waiting to welcome us. The next day, I shared a photo on Instagram with the following caption:

> Arrived last night around 9:30 South Africa time to no less than TEN PEOPLE welcoming us at the airport with dancing and handmade signs. I took one look and bawled my eyes out. Five years of missing these people welled up inside me all at once and now I'm blinking back tears again even as [I] type this, thinking about how blessed we are to be so loved on both sides of the ocean. I don't care what I said in my book [*A Place to Land*] about the food or the beauty of Cape Town … it's all about the people, you guys. Last night God showed me a tiny glimpse of what

> that glorious homecoming will be like one day when His people are united in glory. And it will be beyond all we can imagine this side of heaven.[77]

Have you ever experienced such a rich welcome? Maybe your spouse is serving in the military, and you've had the opportunity to do the welcoming when he or she returned home. I can only imagine the joy, delight, and relief of such a homecoming. Yet any earthly joy we may experience at these events will pale in comparison to the *rich welcome* that God's children will receive when they go home.

As Jen Pollock Michel explains, "The biblical narrative begins and ends at home. From the Garden of Eden to the New Jerusalem we are hardwired for place and for permanence, for rest and refuge, for presence and protection. We long for home because welcome was our first gift of grace and it will be our last."[78]

According to Jerry Bridges,

> There will be no slipping in the side door of heaven with our head hanging down and, to use a popular idiom, our tail between our legs. No, no, a thousand times no! Everyone who has been the object of God's calling and election will receive a rich welcome into Christ's eternal kingdom, not because we deserve it, but because we have been clothed with the spotless robe of Christ's righteousness. It will be because we are united to Him who is the object of the Father's

> everlasting love and delight that we also will be received as objects of His love and delight.[79]

Our earthly nature will whisper lies that death is the end. Truly, it is only the beginning. Only when we get to heaven will the wanderings of painful toil, heartaches, and heartbreaks be over, and believers finally be home.

May the final verses of the Scriptures make us alive with hope for our own homegoing:

"He who testifies to these things says, 'Yes, I am coming soon.'

Amen. Come, Lord Jesus.

The grace of the Lord Jesus be with God's people. Amen" (Rev. 22:20-21 NIV).

QUESTION FOR REFLECTION

When you imagine the welcome you will receive in glory, what is at the forefront of your mind?

ENDNOTES

1 John Piper, *God Is the Gospel: Meditations on God's Love as the Gift of Himself* (Crossway, 2008).

2 Elyse Fitzpatrick, *Home: How Heaven and the New Earth Satisfy Our Deepest Longings* (Bloomington, MN: Bethany House Publishers, 2016), 166.

3 L. M. Montgomery, *Anne of Green Gables: Introduction by Jack Zipes* (New York, NY: The Modern Library, 2008), XX.

4 J. C. Ryle, "Home at Last!," sermon, https://www.truthaccordingtoscripture.com/documents/sermons/home-at-last.php.

5 St. Augustine, *Confessions*, trans. F. J. Sneed (Indianapolis: Hackett Publishing Company, 2006), 3.

6 Glenna Marshall, *The Promise Is His Presence: Why God Is Always Enough* (Phillipsburg, NJ: P&R Publishing, 2019), 177.

7 Rebecca Tekautz, "When Happy Trumps Holy," *Relevant Magazine*, September 10, 2012, http://www.relevantmagazine.com/god/practical-faith/when-happy-trumps-holy.

8 Elyse Fitzpatrick, *Home: How Heaven and the New Earth Satisfy Our Deepest Longings* (Bloomington, MN: Bethany House Publishers, 2016), 161.

9 Charles Spurgeon, "April 25 Morning Devotion," *Morning and Evening: Updated Language Edition* (Grand Rapids, MI: Discovery House, 2016).

10 J. C. Ryle, "Home at Last!," sermon, https://www.truthaccordingtoscripture.com/documents/sermons/home-at-last.php.

11 Sarah Dewberry, "Unaccompanied 6-year-old child put on wrong Spirit Airlines flight," *CNN*, December 25, 2023, https://www.cnn.com/2023/12/24/travel/spirit-airlines-6-year-old-wrong-flight/index.html.

12 Ben Cost, "Man plans trip to Sydney, Australia — ends up in Sidney, Montana," *New York Post*, February 6, 2023, https://nypost.com/2023/02/06/mans-trip-to-sydney-australia-ends-up-in-sidney-montana/.

13 Pallab Ghosh, "Flight and Travel Fears: Why Iceland's Reykjanes Volcano Eruption Won't Cause Disruption," BBC (19 December 2023), https://www.bbc.com/news/science-environment-67762273.

14 Jaide Timm-Garcia, et al., "'Just shocking': Delta passengers tell of airport agony and honeymoon travel woes during tech meltdown," *CNN*, July 25, 2024, https://www.cnn.com/2024/07/25/business/passengers-delta-meltdown-stories/index.html.

15 Jen Pollock Michel, *Keeping Place: Reflections on the Meaning of Home* (Downers Grove, IL: IVP, 2017), 206.

16 C. H. Spurgeon, *Morning and Evening: Updated Language Edition* (Grand Rapids, MI: Discovery House, 2016), 572.

17 John Bunyan, *The Pilgrim's Progress*, excerpt published at Ligonier.org on May 20, 2021, https://www.ligonier.org/learn/articles/christian-loses-his-burden-at-the-cross.

18 Randy Alcorn, *Heaven* (South Africa: Christian Art Publishers, 2004), 10.

19 Ibid.

20 Timothy Lane and Paul Tripp, *Relationships: A Mess Worth Making* (Greensboro, NC: New Growth Press, 2006).

21 Randy Alcorn, *In Light of Eternity* (Colorado Springs, CO: Waterbrook Press, 2009), 6.

22 C. S. Lewis, *The Last Battle* (New York, NY: HarperCollins, 1984), 210.

23 Joni Eareckson Tada, *Heaven: Your Real Home* (Grand Rapids, MI: Zondervan, 1995), 15.

24 Arthur Bennett, ed., *The Valley of Vision: A Collection of Puritan Prayers & Devotions* (Edinburgh, Scotland: The Banner of Truth Trust, 1975), 205. From the poem, "Retrospect and Prospect.".

25 Randy Alcorn, *In Light of Eternity* (Colorado Springs, CO: Waterbrook Press, 2009), 148.

26 Randy Alcorn, *We Shall See God: Charles Spurgeon's Classic Devotional Thoughts on Heaven* (Carol Stream, IL: Tyndale House Publishers, 2011), 193.

27 Jen Pollock Michel, *Keeping Place: Reflections on the Meaning of Home* (Downers Grove, IL: IVP, 2017), 201-202.

28 Joni Eareckson Tada, *Heaven: Your Real Home* (Grand Rapids, MI: Zondervan, 1995), 112.

29 E. M. Bounds, *Heaven — A Place, A City, A Home* (Grand Rapids, MI: Baker Book House, 1975), 125.

30 *Brooklyn*, directed by John Crowley (BBC films, 2015).

31 "10 Key Bible Verses on Sanctification," *Crossway.org*, November 5, 2023, https://www.crossway.org/articles/10-key-bible-verses-on-sanctification/.

32 Jen Wilkin, "Session 5: Sibling Rivalry," video teaching, *God of Covenant: A Study of Genesis 12-50* (Brentwood, TN: Lifeway Press, 2019).

33 Edgar A. Guest, "Home," *A Heap O' Livin'* (Chicago, IL: Reilly & Lee Company, 1916).

34 Andrew M. Davis, *An Infinite Journey* (Greenville, SC: Ambassador International, 2014), 235.

35 Jackie Hill Perry, Jasmine Holmes, and Melissa Kruger. *Ephesians: A Study of Faith and Practice* (Brentwood, TN: Lifeway Press, 2024), 25.

36 Matt Chandler, *The Explicit Gospel* (Wheaton, IL: Crossway Books, 2012), 158.

37 C. S. Lewis, *Mere Christianity* (New York, NY: Macmillan Publishing, 1943), 119.

38 Kara Tippetts, *The Hardest Peace: Expecting Grace in the Midst of Life's Hard* (Colorado Springs, CO: David C. Cook, 2014), 104.

39 John MacArthur, *The Glory of Heaven: The Truth about Heaven, Angels and Eternal Life* (Wheaton, IL: Crossway Books, 1996), 50.

40 Ibid., 55.

41 E. M. Bounds, *Heaven — A Place, A City, A Home* (Grand Rapids, MI: Baker Book House, 1921), 128.

42 Jon Bojer, *The Emigrants,* trans. A. G. Jayne (Denmark: Saga Egmont, 1924, 2022).

43 John MacArthur, *The Glory of Heaven: The Truth about Heaven, Angels and Eternal Life* (Wheaton, IL: Crossway Books, 1996), 49.

44 Nancy Guthrie, "Session 8: The Story of a Dwelling Place," video teaching from the series, "Even Better Than Eden," November 5, 2018, https://vimeo.com/299113507.

45 Ibid.

46 "Heaven," Sermon illustrations, http://www.sermonillustrations.com/a-z/h/heaven.htm.

47 Randy Alcorn, *The Treasure Principle: Unlocking the Secret of Joyful Giving* (Sisters, OR: Multnomah Publishers, 2001), 44-45.

48 Amanda Held Opelt, "Heaven Is A Homeplace," *Christianity Today*, October 8, 2024, https://www.christianitytoday.com/2024/10/heaven-is-a-homeplace-hurricane-helene-appalachia/.

49 Amanda Held Opelt, "Heaven Is A Homeplace."

50 Mark Chanski, "Don't Throw It All Away" sermon, Harbor Reformed Baptist Church, Holland, MI, December 29, 2013.

51 Randy Alcorn, *Heaven* (South Africa: Christian Art Publishers, 2004), 440.

52 Ibid., 78.

53 Kate Motaung, *A Place to Land: A Story of Longing and Belonging* (Grand Rapids, MI: Discovery House Publishers, 2018), 51-53.

54 C. S. Lewis, *Mere Christianity,* 119.

55 Richard Leonard and JoNancy Linn Sundberg, eds. *A Glimpse of Heaven: Through the Eyes of C.S. Lewis, Dr. Tony Evans, Calvin Miller, Randy Alcorn, J. Oswald Sanders, John Wesley, and Others* (Howard Books, 2007), 41.

56 Jen Pollock Michel, *Keeping Place: Reflections on the Meaning of Home* (Westmont, IL: IVP, 2017), 199-200.

57 Ibid., 203.

58 Helen H. Lemmel, "Turn Your Eyes Upon Jesus," Hymn, 1922.

59 Jackie Hill Perry (@jackiehillperry), TikTok video, June 19, 2024, https://www.tiktok.com/@jackiehillperry/video/7382247485537832222.

60 Richard Leonard and JoNancy Linn Sundberg, eds. *A Glimpse of Heaven: Through the Eyes of C.S. Lewis, Dr. Tony Evans, Calvin Miller, Randy Alcorn, J. Oswald Sanders, John Wesley, and Others* (Howard Books, 2007), 45-46.

61 Virginia Sorensen, *Miracles on Maple Hill* (New York, NY: Harcourt, Brace, Jovanovich, 1956), 27.

62 Joni Eareckson Tada, *Heaven: Your Real Home* (Grand Rapids, MI: Zondervan, 1995), 126.

63 Randy Alcorn, *Heaven* (South Africa: Christian Art Publishers, 2004), 77.

64 E.M. Bounds, *Heaven — A Place, A City, A Home* (Grand Rapids, MI: Baker Book House, 1975), 127.

65 C. S. Lewis, *The Weight of Glory, and Other Addresses* (New York, NY: Harper Collins, 1976), 26.

66 Arthur Bennett, ed., *The Valley of Vision: A Collection of Puritan Prayers & Devotions* (Edinburgh, Scotland: The Banner of Truth Trust, 1975), 203. From the poem, "Earth and Heaven."

67 Arthur Bennett, ed., *The Valley of Vision: A Collection of Puritan Prayers & Devotions* (Edinburgh, Scotland: The Banner of Truth Trust, 1975), 204. From the poem, "Heaven Desired."

68 "What Heaven is Like," Sermon illustration, *Ministry 127*, https://ministry127.com/resources/illustrations/heaven.

69 Ian Turner "How to Hold a Living Hope," sermon, Harbor Reformed Baptist Church, Holland, MI, April 2, 2017, sermonaudio.com/sermon/47172125510 (19:39).

70 Ibid., (17:03).

71 "The Cape of Good Hope," Sermon illustration, *Ministry 127*, https://ministry127.com/resources/illustrations/heaven.

72 Glenna Marshall, *The Promise is His Presence: Why God is Always Enough* (Phillipsburg, NJ: P&R Publishing, 2019), 182-183.

73 Timothy Keller, *Walking with God through Pain and Suffering* (New York, NY: The Penguin Group, 2013), 313-314.

74 Kate Motaung (@katemotaung), Instagram post, September 22, 2024, https://www.instagram.com/katemotaung/p/DAO3F1_Sszm/.

75 Eyewitness News, "Man falls 650 feet from NYC Marathon finish line, carried across by other runners," *ABC 7 NY*, November 8, 2021, https://abc7ny.com/runners-stop-to-help-man-held-up-across-finish-line-trio-crosses-nyc-marathon-2021/11211592/.

76 Richard Leonard and JoNancy Linn Sundberg, eds. *A Glimpse of Heaven: Through the Eyes of C.S. Lewis, Dr. Tony Evans, Calvin Miller, Randy Alcorn, J. Oswald Sanders, John Wesley, and Others* (Howard Books, 2007), 75.

77 Kate Motaung (@katemotaung), Instagram post, June 10, 2018, https://www.instagram.com/p/Bj1zo8jAmFy/.

78 Jen Pollock Michel, *Keeping Place: Reflections on the Meaning of Home* (Westmont, IL: IVP, 2017), 33.

79 Jerry Bridges, *The Gospel for Real Life* (Colorado Springs, CO: Navpress, 2002), 165-166.

ABOUT THE AUTHOR

Kate Motaung is the award-winning author of *Letters to Grief* (2025 ECPA Christian Book Award Winner), *101 Prayers for Comfort in Difficult Times*, and the memoir, *A Place to Land: A Story of Longing and Belonging*. She and her husband have three young adult children and currently live in West Michigan. Connect with Kate at katemotaung.com or find her at fiveminutefriday.com.